From Atoms to Angels

From Atoms
to Angels

The Spiritual Forces Shaping Your Life

PAUL D. WALSH-ROBERTS

Gateway

Gateway
an imprint of
Gill & Macmillan Ltd
Hume Avenue
Park West
Dublin 12
with associated companies throughout the world
www.gillmacmillan.ie

0 7171 3088 6

Print origination by O'K Graphic Design, Dublin

Illustrations by Alanna Corballis

Printed by The Guernsey Press, Guernsey

A catalogue record is available for this book from the British Library.

1 3 5 4 2

*This book is dedicated
to all of those courageous souls
who choose to illuminate the path of change
for all on our planet,
with their own unique radiance.
Stay in the Light.*

CONTENTS

Author's note		ix
Acknowledgements		xi
1	Reality	1
2	Purpose	8
3	Separation	18
4	Creation	28
5	Synchronicity	38
6	Power	47
7	Love	55
8	Responsibility	62
9	Healing	70
10	Life force	79
11	Mastery	90
12	Reunion	101
13	Fulfilment	112

AUTHOR'S NOTE

Throughout the developed world, increasingly great numbers of people are beginning to question the dynamic and direction of their life and that of our planet.

This book represents stimulus to those who are no longer prepared to take a passive role in the way they live, but instead are seeking alternative experience as well as meaningful responses to the increasing tide of questions and dissatisfactions.

From Atoms to Angels addresses the most fundamental issues behind this search and crystallises them into tools which can be used in day-to-day life by anyone who chooses. These may contradict, stretch and defy personal boundaries of comfort and ease, but that does not invalidate them. They work. Encapsulating in an exceedingly simplified form what can only be described as the most vast of subjects, *From Atoms to Angels* presents concepts which challenge conventional thinking and serve to expand existing perspectives, creating the real makings of a totally new world that is tangibly fulfilling for one and all. Therefore, by intent and necessity it moves beyond established understanding, belief systems and structures, feeling no need to contradict the *status quo*, nor defend its own substance.

It is my heartfelt intention to aid and support all those who are now in search of greater understanding, choice and responsibility within their existing life. We don't have to look at our world the way we have been told: we do have choices. This book presents the basis of them. You can make them any time you wish, and applying them will set you and the rest of humanity free to be fulfilled. The examples in this book are mostly my personal experience; others are gained from friends or from situations people have cited during workshops I was facilitating.

I have come to see that, world wide, there is now an almost overwhelming sense of the profound changes that we are moving into, and it is only those who allow themselves to see our world through different eyes that will find and lead the way out of the maze of uncertainty and difficulty that prevails on our planet.

The truths this book presents facilitate the realisation, understanding and acceptance of the profound doorway at which each and every one of us has arrived.

If I may ask one thing of my reader, it is that you approach *From Atoms to Angels* with an open heart, enjoy the journey and ask yourself honestly where you fit in.

Paul D. Walsh-Roberts

ACKNOWLEDGEMENTS

Many beautiful souls who I have encountered along my path have nudged, cajoled, pressured or encouraged me to write this book. For me, they have manifested all around the globe as those who have seen themselves as my loved ones or my challenges, and many variations in between. They will know who they are, and will understand that I know also. My unconditional love and thanks go out to each and every one of you.

To my divine 'inspirators' and mentors in Light, I offer deep gratitude. Every breath I take brings more of their guidance and love. Without their subtle (and frequently not-so-subtle!) influence, I may never have even begun writing at all, let alone this book. They have ensured that I have stepped out of my comfort zone at the perfect moments in the perfect ways, even when I disagreed. They have provided me with unlimited support and understanding from near and far, usually in ways that I could never have imagined until it actually became my reality.

Through sheer intimacy, divine synchronicity, mental and emotional strength and courage — not to mention an indescribable flood of unconditional love — the most profound support has been my wife, Alexandria. She has moved me, guided and inspired me in extraordinary ways, often at such depths that I am sure neither of us fully realises. Through all manner of my own resistance, denial and avoidance concerning my own healing, and my writing and her crucial editing of this book, she has been unwaveringly truthful, loving and enlightening. Without her efforts woven throughout, this book would not exist. With this extraordinary woman I am blessed to experience all that lies within these pages. And we do. I could never have imagined what was in store through learning and experiencing such unconditional love.

Thank you from the very centre of my being.

Paul

Chapter 1

▲

REALITY

It is natural for people to look about themselves at all that is in their lives, and overlook the fact that the way the world appears is not actually the way it is. Our world is a wonderful, malleable one — an illusion with unlimited potential, constantly changing, transforming and evolving. It is 'energy-putty' in our hands.

When did you last lie back and watch beautiful, soft, fluffy white clouds waft across the sky on a breezy summer day? They are an intriguing sight, changing shape constantly, creating hints of faces, objects, animals and birds; revealing all manner of beauty in every passing moment.

Each cloud, although appearing to be so light, is actually made up of hundreds, or even thousands of tonnes of individual droplets of moisture, all of which move constantly to form the shapes and images that are so fascinating. Due to both its movement and size, each individual droplet is invisible to the naked eye. But get enough of them together at one time in one place and, by the magic of nature, there it is — the wispy white cloud. A collection of tiny, weightless, invisible things becomes big, heavy and visible.

It's all a matter of density. The more tiny water droplets that gather, the less space and movement they have; the denser the cloud gets, the blacker it looks and the heavier it becomes. Before you know it, the wispy white cloud has become a thick opaque mass. Our entire universe forms in the same way.

Energy focuses into ultra-tiny particles of light that form the atoms of which our world is constructed. The atoms are attracted to each other, their movement becoming increasingly limited by the closeness of their neighbouring atoms. This creates even denser, bigger, heavier particles of energy which are further limited in their movement. These invisible energy particles continue to gather together until their condensed form becomes visible to the naked eye, even tangible. This is what creates the illusion of substances.

Water is one kind of particle that commonly appears in different forms due to density. At very low temperatures, water particles are close together, vibrating within limited distances at relatively low speeds. This very dense state of the water particles appears to the human eye as solid form — ice. If they begin to speed up, each particle uses more space to move, raising the frequency of its vibrations and creating a less-dense, liquid form — water. When the particles take up still more space and vibrate at even higher speeds, they create steam — an even less-dense, gaseous form. In all of these states — ice, water and steam; solid liquid and gas — the particles themselves are exactly the same. Only their state and appearance differ, determined by the way they are using, or expressing, energy as movement (Figure 1.1). This movement is vibration. The rate of vibration is the frequency of the energy. Together, density and frequency determine the innumerable forms that the fundamental energy appears to take in our world.

Figure 1.1

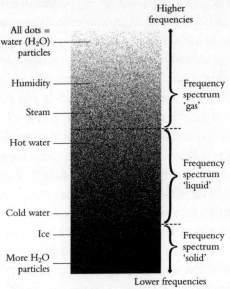

These forms occupy space, and their activity in the world takes time. A simple flower occupies space and time to grow and blossom, just as a child occupies space and time to grow and play and evolve into adulthood, learning to appreciate the beauty of the flower. Together, space and time permeate our entire universe, continually interacting in a seamless eternity called a space–time continuum.

Though much of it seems to be so static, solid and unalterable, our entire space–time universe is malleable like play-dough. This 'softness' is by virtue of the fact that the invisibly small energy particles are actually moving invisibly fast, perpetually changing location and speed. They just slow down to become dense groups of particles which we see and experience in a particular spot, then accelerate out into the higher speeds again, only to be replaced by other slowing particles.

Vibrating in and out of physical density, entering and leaving form in such high frequency and quantity, their collective activity appears to be static. It sets up a visible 'blur' like a mirage which we perceive as material substance. So the forms we see are not really solid or static, just a mirage of innumerable particles constantly slowing down then speeding up again, with us perceiving them only at their slowest speeds (Figure 1.2).

There is a particular limit of speed below which the energy particles must be in order to participate in our space–time universe at all. Only when they slow down enough can we detect and experience them as the objects and substances they form. That threshold of slower movement is called the 'speed of light', and establishes the highest limit of our space–time universe (and the 'glass ceiling' of accepted scientific endeavour in our world). Of course, when the energy moves at rates beyond the limits of human perception, it is not a part of our 'experienceable' physical universe. Hence, we don't notice it, relate to it, or even think of it as 'real', simply because it is outside our reality.

Reality

Reality is simply an environment combined with experience of it. It is the reality of whomever or whatever is experiencing the environment.

Figure 1.2

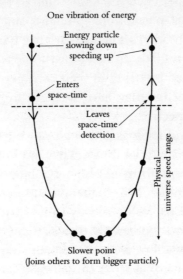

One vibration of energy

Energy particle
slowing down
speeding up

Enters
space-time

Leaves
space-time
detection

Physical
universe speed range

Slower point
(Joins others to form bigger particle)

Our space–time universe, combined with human experience of it, constitutes humankind's reality. It is not the only reality, just the one of which we humans are aware. Birds and animals, insects and bacteria, rocks and plants and substances each have their own realities based on their experience of their portion of this universe. We are unaware of what their experience is like, just as they are of ours. Nonetheless, bird reality, frog reality, tree reality, cellular reality, rock reality, and all the other realities are just as real as each other, and they co-exist within the space–time continuum along with human reality.

Within human reality, every individual person's life is their own individual reality. What is real for you is not necessarily real for me, or anyone else, because no two people ever experience the same thing in the same way. Their individual perceptions, thoughts and feelings are different to each other's. Their experience is unique. Their concept of life is made up of all the thoughts and feelings which are gained by being in their own personal version of every experience they have, seeing it from their own individual perspective.

Thoughts and feelings, although not physical, are the same energy as material things. They are just the energy taking a different form — higher vibrations than the physical spectrum. Their higher vibrations make them more fluid and malleable and dynamic than solid things like bricks; or our bodies, for that matter. Our thoughts, feelings and sensations are our personal awareness of life. They enable each of us to be conscious of our experience in our physical world.

Life is conscious experience. They are one and the same.

Since these higher vibrations of energy enable us to be conscious of life, then it follows that as the vibrations of energy rise even higher, the more we gain conscious experience of life. That means more of all the things that life is made of — more sensory information, more variety, more potential and more 'of it' (increased longevity).

Absolutely every feeling, sensation, thought and observation we are conscious of receiving through our own senses in every single experience, adds to our own individual state of being conscious — our conscious-ness.

Consciousness is the universe and all it contains. It is both the environment and the experience of the environment. Consciousness is reality.

The very energy that makes up all that is physical and non-physical, high or low frequency, is the same thing — light. It is the energy of sensation, awareness and understanding of life experience; plus it is the energy of all that is tangible. We are made of it, and we live it. It is us, and it is our lives and everything in them.

Moving into higher consciousness is the key to gaining not only a higher degree of understanding of life, but also extended life and a greater menu of life experiences from which to choose. It widens our awareness and sensory perception to include much more than the limited spectrum to which we have become accustomed.

How limited or unlimited anyone perceives their life is simply a matter of the particular frequency, or level of consciousness, which they most readily maintain. Furthermore, if the energy was to rise in its overall frequency throughout our entire world, then everyone's lives would become extended, as well as offer a greater menu of life experiences. This would do away with apparent limited options and qualities, and limiting sensations. Everyone would have the opportunity to experience totally different kinds of lives.

Chapter 2

▲

PURPOSE

We are not here to learn nor be happy or unhappy, and we don't have to try to become anything we're not already. We're just here to experience. As long as we allow the flow of experience to come to us, everything will fall into place naturally, in due course. Peace, wisdom and fulfilment will be the result.

Our reality is just one spectrum of vibrations within the infinitely high and infinitely low span of 'All-That-Is' — the all-pervasive, all-creative energy that is the consciousness that understands, knows, experiences and is everything.

The flow of the energy of All-That-Is descends from the highest vibrations into a series of lower and lower worlds of experience called dimensional realities; or simply realms, or dimensions. Each dimension contains its own spectrum of vibrations, and the lower its spectrum, the more limited the original energy has become. This lowering of energy is characterised by more individualised types of life, experience and expression, such as separate beings or life forms, with individual characteristics, feelings and sensations.

Together, the dimensions are like the floors of a multi-storey building. Each floor contains a different layer of experience pertaining to its own spectrum of consciousness frequencies. The cosmic elevator of descension and ascension enables the consciousness, or energy, to step down and up to lower and higher levels of experience and awareness (Figure 2.1).

Within the infinite spectrum of energy vibrations, our physical space–time universe contains the portion that is low enough to support material form and solidity. This portion of the spectrum is referred to as the 'third dimension'. This does not mean 'dimension' in the conventional sense of height, width or length. Rather, ours is called the third dimension because it has just three components by which we are empowered to experience life and thereby understand ourselves and our state of consciousness. That is to say, it provides three ways by which we may be conscious, rather than being unconscious.

Figure 2.1

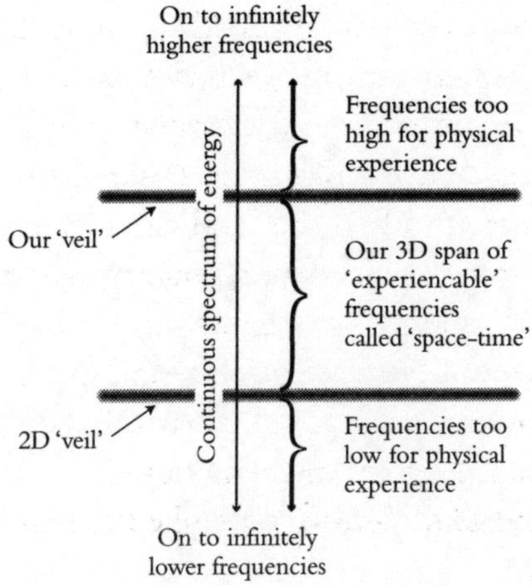

On to infinitely higher frequencies

Frequencies too high for physical experience

Our 'veil'

Our 3D span of 'experiencable' frequencies called 'space-time'

2D 'veil'

Frequencies too low for physical experience

Continuous spectrum of energy

On to infinitely lower frequencies

The lowest, most dense of the three consciousness components is physical — the manifested, neutral energy by which a physical world actually exists for us to experience. The next higher spectrum is emotional — the negative, receptive, passive (feminine) energy by which we receive sensory information and feel our reality. The highest level by which 3D consciousness functions is the mental — the positive, projective, active (masculine) energy by which we project our beliefs and personalities into our world, directing our physical, emotional and mental actions. (In this context, positive and negative do not equate with good and bad, just as the feminine and masculine principals are not weak and strong. They are like the terminals on any battery, or in an electric power socket — both are necessary to make energy usable.)

The 'densities' of mental, emotional and physical energies affect us directly every day. Consider how easy it

Figure 2.2

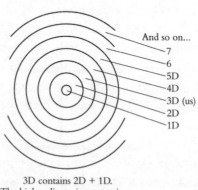

And so on...
7
6
5D
4D
3D (us)
2D
1D

3D contains 2D + 1D.
The higher dimensions contain us

is to change your mind about something, how much more difficult it is to alter your feelings about it, and how seemingly impossible it can be to change the physical form itself.

These three dimensions are all we have, as long as we contain our own consciousness within their bounds by choosing to see life only in mental, emotional and physical terms. They are not our only capabilities — we are just limited to them, and to the experiences they enable us to have. Each of these three components is unlimited in its potential, and we can use all or any of them to any extent or in any way we so choose, according to our own free will. This can be to our detriment or to our benefit, but we choose it to be so.

The way we choose to acknowledge these three faculties and use them to their maximum or partial potential, perpetually determines the basis of our conscious experience and our understanding of life. If we use only a limited version of these tools, then we experience only a limited version of life's potential and gain only limited understanding of it. Until we are able and willing to entertain alternative ways of perceiving life, or other ways of working with these tools, we will be limited to the third-dimensional experiences and the types of limited realities to which we have become accustomed.

Each lower dimension is actually contained within, and permeated by, the higher ones (Figure 2.2). If you were to move into a lower dimension, that would remove one facet of consciousness from your control. Each higher dimension would offer you one more facet; another tool that you could use at will. Looking at our neighbouring dimensions, second-dimensional consciousness loses the ability to generate original thought, its inhabitants being conscious only of sensing their world and responding to it by instinct alone. Conversely, fourth-dimensional consciousness adds the aspect of time within its command, which its inhabitants can mould to create experience such as time travel.

Lower dimensions can be aware of the higher influences, depending upon their sensitivity to the higher frequency energies, but they are unable to utilise or make sense of them until their consciousness expands to contain them as new tools. We in the third dimension are aware of time as an influence upon our experience, but it seems to be beyond our control. Higher up the scale are even subtler influences which, in our lower-frequency consciousness, we are unable to sense at all. They still permeate our reality, but we will only sense them and utilise them when we raise our own consciousness frequency to come into resonance with them, or raise our acceptance levels to receive their 'wavelength'.

As a result, in second-dimensional consciousness, we would experience life as a constant stream of instinctive response and adaptation to circumstances that seemed to be happening to us. Conversely, in fourth-dimensional consciousness we'd have extra experience and understanding gained from the ability to mould time, the way we are presently able to control only thought, emotion and physical form. This is why, if we lower our own consciousness, we feel as though much of life is beyond our control. It is not actually beyond our control, we have simply disallowed ourselves from fully utilising the three tools that are already at our disposal, and are unlimited.

Our dimension is unique in that its three-faceted basis of awareness, or picture of life, makes it the lowest dimension that can support fully-conscious beings who experience by free will. We are beings free to choose what to think and feel and experience in life. This absolute freedom is available to us only when all three aspects of the third-dimensional consciousness are fully active in us. When we choose to lower our consciousness by ignoring or forgetting their potential, we once again feel unable to control life's events.

Ultimately, this means that we are all experiencing our own reality of our own free will. What is more, we are experiencing it in the way we choose, albeit using only the most limited combination of tools to accomplish the job.

That we choose to experience life in this physical dimension makes humanity unique. We are the portion of the consciousness of All-That-Is that volunteered to experience physical life and its inherent limitations. As physical beings, we are vital in the gathering of experience in the physical universe so that the all-embracing consciousness that is All-That-Is can indeed be all that there is, which includes the physical part.

Our divine purpose in being has always been to experience life in the physical dimension. It's not vague or mysterious at all; it's very simple. The more thoroughly we experience, without hesitation or resistance, through our actions, feelings and thoughts, the more we are fulfilling our spiritual path, our divine purpose.

The forms of life inhabiting other dimensions volunteer to gather different kinds of experience which relate to their own spectrum of consciousness, be it higher or lower. That is their essential purpose in fulfilling and being their part of All-That-Is. So we are not alone in our journey. We are hand-in-hand with the beings in neighbouring dimensions, together creating a continuous chain of consciousness in which every single one of us is a vital link. This chain enables the flow of consciousness throughout the dimensions, and it is managed very carefully. Each dimension has responsibilities to be met by its own guardians. These guardians are the beings that inhabit and experience their particular dimension. They manage the energy flow so that their dimension's consciousness (their reality and state of being) can be sustained by the influx of the higher energy of the next dimension up the chain. Similarly, their consciousness is required to support and nourish the continuity of life experience by passing on their energy to the lower dimensions.

In our third dimension, these guardians are us — humankind. Our responsibilities as guardians of our dimension are, first, to allow the consciousness of the higher dimensions to flow into our lives; and second, to utilise and pass on that energy in support of the wildlife, plant and mineral kingdoms.

The whole purpose of this chain of creation is to provide continual nourishment and life support that will enable ongoing experience to be gathered in all ways in all dimensions so that All-That-Is can encapsulate and be it all. Lower dimensions are enabled by higher ones to experience life and subsequently serve a 'higher' purpose, though they may not be consciously aware of it.

If a dimension gained direct exposure to the next higher dimension's frequencies, then just as steam dissolves ice, their experience of their version of life would also be dissolved. In order that their version of life may continue in the degree of limitation they had chosen, every dimension has a threshold, or veil, at its highest boundary. It acts as a filter to prevent direct contact with adjacent dimensions.

This veil is able to move higher and lower. It moves higher according to the increasing capability, or willingness, of the lower dimension to embrace and utilise higher frequency energy without disabling their own world of experience. It moves lower according to the decreasing ability, or resistance, of the lower dimension to embrace the higher consciousness.

And so, to be absolutely everything, the all-knowing, all-understanding, omnipresent consciousness that is All-That-Is progressively stepped down from the awareness of absolute unlimitedness and unity, through this system of self-limitation. It became increasingly individualised streams of consciousness as it poured through lowering dimensions, eventually creating the physical version of life. In order to gather and be conscious of the countless possibilities of physical experience, enough of these separate, individualised streams of consciousness were required to form and be active in the physical realm (Figure 2.3).

Figure 2.3

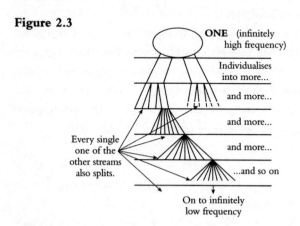

Enter us — humanity. We were perfect. As we passed through the veil, we became these individualised physical beings we see ourselves to be. We stepped away from our higher consciousness and knowledge which remained back beyond the veil. Separating from our previously held knowledge meant we allowed ourselves to forget our inter-dimensional capabilities, our higher consciousness and unlimitedness, and our knowledge of unity with all that is. We did so in order to truly experience the limitation of being physical. If we actually recalled how unlimited and omnipotent we truly are, our present experience of limitation would simply not be possible. It would be like a jet pilot trying to fly by feathering his arms and flapping them — he simply wouldn't bother because he knows better. In that case, neither would our divine purpose be possible to fulfil. The entire chain of continuously limiting dimensional realities that enable us to exist, would collapse.

In such a way, we disconnected from our origins as part of the higher realms and began to live the denial of our true, complete, powerful, multi-dimensional selves through our newly acquired aspect of consciousness called ego. We came into our experience of separateness from our origins — from that 'home' frequency.

Chapter 3

▲

SEPARATION

Ego is the part of us that maintains the belief that our physical embodiment and physical surroundings are all that is. Believing it is separate from every one and every thing, it defends, mollycoddles, preens and projects itself in its attempts to feel safe and good enough. Finally, ego suffocates physical embodiment by fear and resistance to the natural flow of life experience, as well as by denial of the very force that enables it to exist.

Coming through the veil into individualised soul identities and personalities, we became separated from our higher consciousness, knowledge and understanding. Consequently, we began to experience the effects of such separation. These effects were a perception of life based on disconnectedness — separation from everything; the apparent loss of any sense of unity. This is the view maintained by ego.

Ego is the part of one's overall consciousness which sees only the separate physical person; separate from other people and from the environment. As a result, it is aware only of the separate individual as different from all other separate individuals. It interprets 'different' as superior or inferior and right or wrong, instead of just different. Therefore, for fear of feeling inadequate or less or worse or wrong, it believes it needs to make itself better or more, or to justify its being exactly who it is. That is why many people think of ego simply as vanity or excessive attention to one's self.

Ego is the living denial of each person's true identity as a perfect individualised image of the divine consciousness that is All-That-Is. There is nothing wrong with ego; it fulfils a crucial purpose in enabling us to experience any degree of limitedness we choose in this dimension of ours. But to do so, ego functions only within the veil of forgetfulness, relating only to the limitations of the physical universe which it sees before it. Through only the crude, elementary physical senses of sight, sound, taste, touch and smell, it feeds and perpetuates its sense of separateness. It also uses those senses to maintain the survival of its physical embodiment through the experiences it has.

In short, ego is the manager of our third-dimensional consciousness vehicle — our physical body. It has simply enabled us to forget our higher self, the soul essence which manages our higher-dimensional consciousness vehicle — our light body. Our higher self is the part of us that connects to higher-frequency consciousness, ensuring that we don't become trapped in physical limitation, irretrievably losing contact with higher knowing and our spiritual guidance.

To illustrate the relationship of these two most fundamental components, imagine for a moment that you are a car. Your ego's view of life is from the headlights only and it operates only the brakes and accelerator, believing that it can ensure security and fulfilment respectively. It actually thinks that what it sees is all that is, and it believes it is in control of the entire journey. But back there at the steering wheel, behind the instrument panel, is your higher self. It has a far greater view. It is able to look all around the situation, as well as see on the instrument panel what systems are in overload and need rest or attention to prevent breakdowns. It also guides the direction by the steering wheel so that the car stays on the road and unnecessary detours can be avoided. What's more, there is another very important item at the disposal of the higher self — the map, which shows exactly where to find the fulfilment and blissful ecstasy that the journey is intended to be reaching. It also shows the quickest and easiest route to take. The higher self also sees all of the signposts, even though some may not be right in front or obvious.

Regardless of how unsatisfactory the view is from the ego's headlight perspective at any given time, it resists changing it for fear of experiencing something unpredictably worse, unsafe or invalidating (the devil it doesn't know). Meanwhile, every time the all-knowing, understanding, wise and loving higher self guides the journey away from the ego's mediocrity (the devil it knows) towards blissful fulfilment (joy, ecstasy, abundance and love), all the ego sees is its view changing. It doesn't like changes at all. It only wants to defend its existing limited but secure bubble of knowledge and experience. It feels the fear of uncertainty setting in and slams on the brakes. The flow stops and life stands still. The whole car then sits there in the middle of the road, immobilised by fear. The tyres flatten slowly and the body deteriorates from disuse, waiting for the ego to release the brakes and get back into the flow of life.

Not until the love of life, the will and longing for fulfilment, becomes strong enough to look outside the limiting view of the headlights, does the journey continue and life begin to flow again.

The original idea was that together, the ego and the higher self would make a great team — our complete spiritual self — for the duration of the great sojourn in the physical dimension. However, through the veil we had created the illusion of being disconnected from everything we truly are, no longer giving any credibility to the quiet inner voice of our higher self. We had each moved into a separated stream of ego-conscious experience. Our tendency to see ourselves only as separate to everyone and everything gave birth to polarity consciousness.

Polarity consciousness is simply being conscious of polarities; that is, being aware only of contrasting or conflicting opposites, with all of life appearing to be drawn into one side of the equation or the other.

Opposites appear to be separate from each other: a winner or a loser, the have's or the have not's, one or the other. In day-to-day life, this means everything appears to be good or bad, and right or wrong, love or hate, yes or no, and endless other subjective opinions. All of them are indeed personal, subjective opinions, and they promote the apparent (not actual) need to choose one or the other in order to remain safe and comfortable. This apparent need creates desire for the most preferred polarity, and resistance to its opposite.

In separating everything in life into one end of the scale or the other in this way, polarity consciousness gave rise to imbalance and disharmony through judgement. Judgement formed according to the ego's desires for 'good', its preference for 'better', the need to validate itself as 'right', protect itself from 'bad' and prove itself not 'wrong'.

Maintaining this judgement was meant to protect the fragile ego from feeling fear, pain, loneliness, uncertainty, struggle, invalidation, scarcity and anything else it judged to be undesirable. But it didn't really matter because All-That-Is (which was all the time flowing in and functioning through our higher selves) had decided it was going to experience absolutely everything this physical density had to offer, and that it would do so by expressing itself through our physical embodiment without limitation or hesitation. And that is all that ego resists when it employs its petulant antics.

Ego is easily identified. When given free reign, it either thinks it is in control or thinks it is powerless; either dominant or a victim of circumstance with 'no choice'. It constantly sends out fearful messages of need — for approval, agreement, control, power, knowledge, validation, safety, security, predictability. This is because it craves to compensate for its belief that the self is not enough, based on the deeply underlying sense of separation from truth, understanding and power, and isolation from its spiritual 'home' and true belonging. This sense of inadequacy craves to be satisfied by dominance or by pity; or by knowing 'the finite facts' about everything so that it can try to control the flow of life and feelings with the help of that knowledge.

Ego projects such conscious and subconscious insecurity messages at an alarming rate. The underlying purpose behind these is to create drama and complication to make the ego and its life appear more interesting, full or important. They take all forms of attention-seeking, such as, 'Is my car OK? How about my hair style? I hope everyone thinks I have a good job. Please think I'm smart. Does she like me? Do you love me? You should like the things I like. Think the things I think. Do what I do. They should do what I say. You shouldn't just do what you want. But he should do this. Why won't she do what I want? Why won't he be how I want him to be? Don't do things that make me feel insecure, nervous or uncomfortable in any way. Please don't choose to feel or do things that I wouldn't like to feel or do.'

In such ways, ego believes it can make itself safe from contradiction; from things it doesn't want to experience because they are wrong or bad or uncomfortable; from powerlessness, pain and struggle; in fact from all forms of insecurity and invalidation. But the further these project outwards, the flimsier they get, and the more it feels pressured to create even more. This is a treadmill that ego perpetuates, and it must go faster and faster to prevent something undesirable, unexpected or unpredictable leaking into its insecurity zone (Figure 3.1).

Figure 3.1

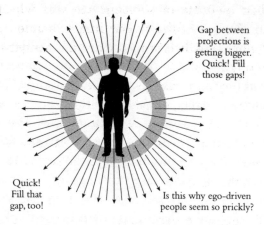

Gap between projections is getting bigger. Quick! Fill those gaps!

Quick! Fill that gap, too!

Is this why ego-driven people seem so prickly?

Ego seeks out all who will come under its spell, magnetising other egos and draining them of life force (we have all felt that from time to time). Like attracts like, and egos attract egos which understand each other's needs and will play the ego game of mutual insecurity, dominator and dominated, taker and giver, leader and follower, chased and pursuer.

In order to maintain the eternal state of natural balance throughout the cosmos, when one ego gets into one polarity, other egos are unwittingly drawn in to fill the opposite end of the scale. The further ego goes out on a polarity limb, the more powerful must be its opposite. For every winner there is a loser. Just as a victim will invariably find a perpetrator, a person being shy and submissive will attract another being dominant and controlling. The ego that desires or hoards a stockpile of plenty is truly afraid of scarcity and inevitably finds itself exposed to poverty in its reality somewhere, sometime, be it their own life or someone else's of which they are aware. And all of the reverse instances automatically are true, none of which bring joy or fulfilment, true peace or harmony.

But the funny thing is that none of this is real. It is all an illusion; a mirage made up of energy that is not even physical. Our egos think things are polarised, and that one end or other of the scale must be favoured, simply because it's the way egos perceive all that is. But it is only true to the ego.

Polarity consciousness is *a* truth, not *the* truth. It is purely subjective, personal truth. It is not objective, divine truth — cosmic law which applies to everyone and everything regardless of opinion. Ego just treats its own view as the truth and tries to control other egos to come into alignment with it. That way, it can have the security of accompaniment on its lonely, separated path through life.

But in actuality, each of us has just been weaving our own personal path of experience through an infinite spectrum of possibilities, all of which are contained within the span of energy vibrations that constitute our particular dimension.

We are not intrinsically incomplete or limited — only our perception of ourselves and our world is incomplete and limited: distorted by fear. We only think our polarity world is all that is and that we need something outside of ourselves to make us happy — that we are powerless and need power, vulnerable and need protection, ignorant and need to be told. It is not truth, only perception.

In this fearful state of polarised perception and denial of our true identity, ego believes fundamentally that it is a victim of the flow of creation and so it needs to be in control to make life safe from discomfort on all levels — physical, emotional and mental. It does so by avoiding uncertainty — resisting unpredictable change.

But what the ego doesn't consider is that the entire universe is already in a perpetual state of change and uncertainty. The very energy particles of which everything is made are constantly changing both speed and position. Our blood flows, and the trees move as the wind blows. The tides are changing, and night and day are displacing each other year in and year out. The Earth is revolving, as is our star system and our galaxy. Our bodies are producing cells as we extract energy from our environment, which is constantly changing around us. How can we hope to control this?

Ego is trying to control and limit the natural function of creation! It is pitting itself against the entire cosmos! A task that is absolutely ridiculous and impossible, not to mention totally unnatural.

Change is the natural flow of creation. So the issue is not one of change or no-change. It is just a matter of where each ego chooses to draw its own personal line of comfort and acceptability through the continuous ocean of potentiality offered through change. That line is its own self-limiting, imaginary threshold which serves only to trap the person in his or her own limited version of life's potential, rather than liberating them into absolute potential.

But the situation is not without hope. We are not actually just ego but truly unlimited, omnipotent beings with an illusory wall of ego-limitation around us. But the wall of ego-consciousness is dissolving as we become more aware of its existence and dare to reach through it to find a more fulfilling experience of life. Simultaneously, all that we have forgotten behind the veil is now returning to empower us once more — primarily the memory and understanding that we are the masters of creation, not the victims.

We each have the power already, and to find it we need look nowhere but within.

Chapter 4

▲

CREATION

All that is in physical reality originates through our own thoughts, based on our underlying beliefs, which focus energy into form. Group thoughts create group reality, just as an individual's thoughts create their personal reality. It is all in the mind, and perpetuating an existing reality or creating a new one is a simple case of mind over matter.

We all have thoughts: our minds are perpetually having them. Some we are consciously aware of, and others we are not. These are determined by our conscious and subconscious attitudes, opinions and preferences. Such persuasions originate from a collection of instinctive and inherited influences, knowledge and understanding. Everyone holds as valid and true a unique blend of these influences which is their own personal underlying belief system. Each person's belief system determines the way they think life is. It does not determine the way life *actually* is.

As well as these individual belief systems, there are collective belief systems to which masses of individuals contribute and by which they are influenced. These include such collectives as cultures, races, religions, histories, ideologies and governments, as well as economic, educational, health and social systems. Such collections of people perpetuate, live by, and often enforce their own particular set of preferences and opinions which they consider acceptable. Yet their limits of acceptability are in fact absolutely arbitrary, being determined only by their ego's own totally subjective belief systems.

Without exception, all beliefs are valid, whether we like and agree with them or not. It is valid for people in certain parts of the world to place their dead relatives on a mountaintop to be picked over by the eagles until the bones are clean and dry. Other cultures may not consider it acceptable, but it is valid by mere virtue of its existence, and its acceptance by those who choose to live by it. Then again, those very people may consider it unacceptable, barbaric and even insulting to the dead relative to just leave the corpse in a box in the ground to rot.

Such differences between the collective belief systems of cultures are most often due to the different influences they experience. These can be as simple as unusual geographical location or extreme weather conditions, or as complex as enforced doctrines or social conditioning.

Nevertheless, people choose to live their lives according to such belief systems. What's more, they will often defend them vehemently, their ego rising to protect itself, demanding validation and craving approval for its differences. And when the ego is collective — such as cultural, national, economic, political, racial or religious — the mechanics of the need for approval are the same, but the manifestations can be devastating, even escalating to war upon those who will not agree.

For the most part, belief systems have become habit, perpetuated without people consciously knowing it. So the values people adhere to and the kind of life they experience are also being perpetuated without them consciously knowing it. This is largely based on the subconscious belief systems ingrained from birth. It's a collection of ideas — seeds of understanding about life, self, values, needs and expectations handed down from one generation of egos to the next, conditioning the open minds of the newborn and training them not to contradict or deviate from the prevailing system of acceptability.

A child born into a family that argues constantly until someone gives in will grow up with an underlying belief that the only way to achieve harmony is through identifying the conflict and winning over the opposition. As they grow, their only experiences of agreement and satisfaction will have been achieved through struggle and confrontation. Likewise, if a child is repeatedly told to be quiet, he or she will develop within their belief system the premise that whenever they speak they will risk disapproval. In this case, they might become timid and non-communicative, even though they have great wisdom to share. This doubt and frustration could easily compound into anger and resentment at a deeper level, one that the person may not even be aware of themselves.

On the other hand, consider a child encouraged in a harmonious environment to value its opinion and itself, no matter how different. It will grow up achieving great confidence easily, since it will tend not to doubt and invalidate itself. It will more likely experience success seemingly automatically due to its underlying belief in a harmonious, supportive reality free of conflict and disallowance. It will also apply similar respect and values to others and enjoy healthy relationships accordingly.

Underlying beliefs are perpetually affecting our thoughts and attitudes about everything. Whether we are aware of it happening or not, those then become the basis of the choices and decisions we make moment by moment, and subsequently what we experience as we weave our own path through life's infinite possibilities.

This is a simple picture of how we function as creators, every one of us 'born in the image of the creator'. We are the creators, and we are living the supremely powerful cosmic game of cause-and-effect, or karma. This is not the punishment or reparation that many have chosen to believe it is. Cause-and-effect and karma are just different names for the same phenomenon — Cosmic Consequence, or the Divine Law of Creation. It simply means that thought (cause) invariably precedes manifested experience (effect). As above (above, meaning the higher frequency of thought energy), so below (below, meaning the lower frequency of energy forming the material world).

Life is happening *through* us; it is not happening *to* us. But when we came through the veil, we forgot that by holding thoughts we mould our experiences. The images in our minds are thought forms — form held in thought.

They are images focused through the lens of our mind, the carrier of all thought, and they precede physical form.

Free will allows us to think whatever we choose to think, about anything and everything. It also allows us to focus however much attention we choose on whichever of those thoughts we choose.

Figure 4.1

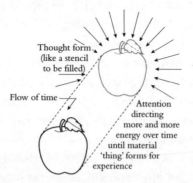

No matter how hard they try, nobody can actually change your mind except you! And nobody can force you to spend your time and efforts thinking about things you choose not to think about. But the attention you give any thought enables the pure energy to focus on it, to gather and densify, and fill the mould with energy particles until eventually the thought form lowers in frequency enough to create physical form (Figure 4.1).

Creation is the flow of life. Life experience is the flow of creation. Creation in our physical world is this system of manifestation through lowering the frequency of thought energy until it enters the physical spectrum to be experienced by physical beings.

Manifestation is thought becoming experience.

Experience can be mental, emotional or physical, but as long as it is in anyone's awareness in any form, it is manifested experience. Whether it is obvious and tangible (experiencing it on our own 'doorstep' of life) or sensory and observational (being aware of it in someone else's life), it is still part of our own reality.

By our own free will, in some way or other, we get to experience whatever we choose to believe or think about.

Even when we have not been consciously aware of it, all of our thoughts have been turning into experience for us. Our ignorance of this has made the very thread of our existence, cause-and-effect, somewhat meaningless and intangible for us. The reasons are manifold. For a start, a vast proportion of thoughts are subconscious, so we are not fully aware of having them. Also, the time it takes for the energy to densify into physical form has been so great (often lifetimes) that we forgot we had the thought in the first place, and the materialised event then appeared to be happening to us. Another very common factor is that we have scattered thoughts, inconsistent in both their subject and its qualities, so the energy cannot find a clear image to which it can anchor itself and densify into form. In this case it becomes a jumbled manifestation, unrecognisable and disowned by its creator. Another very common case is experiencing manifestations that we believe we would never have intended; which is due to our thinking mostly about the things we didn't want. All this creates the common reality combined of both desirable things and undesirable things.

The energy will not over-ride our free will. It assumes that what we are thinking about is exactly what we want. It then lovingly and faithfully adheres to the thought form, or mind picture, not the 'want/don't want' scenario of ego.

All-That-Is does not relate to ego except through us, since we are that arm of its creation for the gathering of 3D experience. It will not make judgements or assumptions on our behalf, nor will it make decisions concerning which of our beliefs or thoughts are best for us, since it is intrinsically neutral and detached. Its only wish is for us to have free will so that we may exercise it with love. It originates in absolute unconditional love — absolute allowance and support of whatever we choose, by our own free will, to think, to experience, to do, to feel and to be. We are the part of it that took responsibility for this dimension of experience on behalf of the whole. We are the manifestations of its thoughts. It is not about to waste energy by duplicating or negating its efforts.

Thoughts can take many forms: logical or intuitive, analytical or creative, fearful or courageous, controlling or allowing, limiting or expansive, aggressive or passive, beautiful or ugly, hateful or loving. Without exception they are the flow of one's consciousness; the flow of the energy of which everything is created with such individuality through each one of us. Fearful thoughts are symptoms of polarity consciousness — expressions of ego, control, need and desire, and the myriad of painful and limiting manifestations of fear. Loving thoughts are symptoms of unity consciousness — expressions of soul, free spirit, allowance and the many joyous and expansive manifestations of love. Fearful thoughts and loving thoughts are just lower and higher frequencies within the spectrum of thought energy.

Nonetheless, thoughts are thoughts, and the time they take to manifest as actual experience is all a matter of what we choose to think about, how clearly we choose to think about it, and how much thought we put into it. In our physical world, the manifestation can be intangible experience, such as sensations and feelings, or it can be an actual tangible, material experience of objects and actions. It will take a substantially more material, tangible form according to the amount of attention the thought has received, and the degree of detachment that is maintained regarding the manifestation.

Take someone who wants a loving relationship. They could experience thus: first, a friend mentions to them that they know someone who has just begun a beautiful new relationship; next they overhear a conversation in a restaurant about another happy new couple; they then notice a magazine article on the subject of quality relationships; a while later they see a couple in the park together, obviously in love. When a family member finds a happy relationship, the manifestation is getting closer than ever to their own experience. The key is to observe these relationships as symbols of the manifestation getting more real for them. Unfortunately, most people treat such observations as symbols that their desires are still being someone else's experience, which is exactly how they then remain. Shift the attitude to detached, neutral observation rather than being emotionally attached to an outcome for oneself.

The flow of creation is inhibited by attachment. This can be attachment to the way in which the object might come into our experience. If it is a fast exotic car which we are wanting, why not allow the flow of creation to bring it in easier ways than by saving and buying it; maybe as a gift from someone, or by unlimited use of the car being offered by an owner, or by winning the money in a lottery? It could come about in such a way, but an existing rigid belief that the only way to get the car would be to earn a large sum of money to pay for it, or that it needs to actually be owned to give pleasure, negates other possibilities. It distracts attention away from the real object and real purpose of the experience, and redirects it towards the issue of money or ownership. It introduces into the equation ego-conscious limitations of self-doubt, struggle and scarcity.

Unfortunately, such alternatives often attract cries of, 'Oh, but that will never happen to me; I'm never that lucky', or 'I had better work harder to get more money more quickly', or 'I need to get more knowledge or education so I can get a better job.' Immediately, that existing belief has put stumbling blocks in the way of the natural flow of creation, which could deliver the car more easily and quickly since it functions with the unlimited potential of the original energy, as long as it is not being redirected into extraneous tasks dreamed up by a fearful, controlling ego. Attachment can also be to actually having the thing; by believing we need it — to make us safe, to make us happy, to make us complete.

Need is the fear of not having. It reinforces the belief that the fulfilling thing which is sought is still outside of self; that there is something 'out there' that will make oneself happy and complete 'in here'. So we keep thinking about it being out there, and it keeps manifesting out there rather than over here with us. The pure intent of the thought form is infected by the belief that the thing is yet unobtained, that it is separate from oneself. Which is exactly how it continues to manifest!

On the other hand, detachment from the outcome acknowledges the object to be already formed in the energy of thought. It removes the infection of separation derived from need, and allows what we desire to densify into physical form and experience in the natural flow of creation — in the cosmically perfect time and form that appears in our lives as synchronicity.

Chapter 5

▲

SYNCHRONICITY

Our universe is held in a perpetual state of delicate balance, with everything in the perfect place, at the perfect time, in the perfect form to ensure each moment's cosmic harmony. It is only us humans with our limited view who think it is anything other than the cosmic dance of perfect creation.

The universe maintains perfect balance, at all times ensuring the perfect timing and form of everything at every point in space and time, and the perfect process of consolidating energy into physicality. It does so by constantly allowing energy to flow through channels which connect imbalances between dimensions, people, situations, manifestations — in fact between every single aspect of the cosmos. If the equilibrium becomes lost, which happens when one polarity is accentuated for some reason, then it automatically becomes balanced by either draining off into the opposite polarity, or by the opposite polarity gaining intensity. This is how we experience a relationship with another person, an object, our life, and our entire world.

Think of it as 'cosmic osmosis'. Just as two rooms, one filled with red mist and the other with blue, will both eventually become filled with purple mist when a doorway is opened between them, so does everything find harmony through interaction. Resist interaction, and you'll perpetuate disharmony. If you walk into a room full of angry people and you are happy, you will inevitably feel the imbalance. If you stay, either you will diminish your level of happiness or they will all become happier. But given time, one way or another everyone will be drawn into a similar emotional state or they will leave the room, dispersing the energy to reform another time for them.

The way you manage the state of harmony throughout your life determines the quality of your relationships and how comfortable they feel for you. You can maintain harmony or you can destroy it. It is your choice. You create your every experience, including those of peacefulness and ease, or of discord and struggle.

It is imperative to understand and accept that you created whatever it is you are experiencing. The understanding comes by simply allowing that idea to be considered in your mind. As it absorbs and settles into your belief system, it will effect an expansion of your view of your reality, and therefore of yourself. By accepting responsibility for the creation, you automatically open yourself to receive higher understanding of the situation. That represents higher consciousness and in due course will reveal the disharmonious beliefs and attitudes that had called for attention by fighting against the universe. As soon as you are capable of assimilating the higher consciousness and understanding, your soul will let it through into your earthly awareness.

This is self-analysis, the discipline of using your free will to advance the frequency of your own consciousness through self-motivated spiritual development and evolution of understanding.

When you experience something that you're inclined to paint with the 'Why me?' whitewash, remember to say 'Oh, I wonder what thoughts I've been having to bring this about?' When you get what you'd been wanting, thank yourself for manifesting it, rather than saying, 'Wow, I don't believe it!' or 'That's incredible!' Believe it! It's totally real! Equally, when you're not getting what you wanted, ask yourself where your thoughts and beliefs have truly been about you having it. If you keep saying it's impossible or it's always someone else's luck, guess what? You create it that way. Own it, be honest with yourself, learn from it, and adjust whatever it is in you that is causing anything less than fulfilment. You are dealing with an orderly process, not a random one.

It is usually easier to attribute an experience to an outside influence rather than to claim responsibility for it yourself and acknowledge the synchronicity in it. Let's say you experience a sore throat. It's easier to say, 'Oh that's because I went out into the cold air from a warm room the other night', or 'I got caught in the rain', than it is to say 'I must have issues with speaking my truth. The fact it has come up now tells me that I have around me at this point in my life the opportunity to resolve it. I'll seek the situation out, and as soon as I address it instead of resisting it, I won't need this symptom and it will fade away.'

You are the one who consciously or subconsciously

decided to go out in the cold, or into a potentially rainy day. Your higher self guided you to the actions you took (forgetting your jacket or not noticing the weather forecast) because it wanted you to get the message about communication issues that need healing before they become a more serious signal, such as laryngitis, or even a cancerous throat condition. You had not become aware of your own tendency to suppress speaking your truth, so its voice had to get louder until you heard. Furthermore, when you begin to discipline yourself to speak your truth all of the time with love, you will find that you never get sore throats, regardless of prevailing conditions.

To see such experience as mere coincidence is to see it as an accidental product of a haphazard or meaningless flow of life. It is the limited ego-self believing it is a mere victim of circumstances, that life is chaotic, and that it is lucky or unlucky according to what is happening to it. This is third-dimensional polarity consciousness — ego-based fearful perception.

To see every experience as synchronicity is to see it as a meaningful product of the natural, harmonious, purposeful flow of life. It is the true soul-self remembering and acknowledging its divine power and purpose as creator by recognising the connectedness of thought and manifestation. This is higher-dimensional love consciousness — soul-based perception. It pushes back the veil of limitation to allow in more conscious understanding. It nourishes one's power, enabling it to blossom more and more with each synchronous instance. That blossoming brings more consciousness and more fulfilling manifestations.

This is being conscious, rather than being asleep to the true reality of life. When people turn to you and say 'Get real', 'Come back to reality' or 'Look at the reality of the situation', you can safely assume they are actually saying, unwittingly, 'Quick, fall asleep like me in case you get a glimpse of the truth of this situation or of yourself.'

It is extremely empowering for you to recognise your every experience as a synchronous reflection of your own consciousness — a symptom of your beliefs and thoughts about yourself, your reality and all that is. This creates a profoundly liberating and exceedingly rich source of information and guidance. Your personal symptoms, be they in your body, mind or feelings, are manifestations of your personal belief system. The environmental symptoms you are aware of, whether they involve you directly or are just observations, are all manifestations of the collective belief system of which you are choosing to be a part.

I believe that a child loses its teeth at an early age, and grows to lose them again in old age, for a very significant reason. Teeth represent our basic belief systems: the means by which we are able to break up the experience of life into bite-size digestible understanding so that it can nourish us and help us gain wisdom through growth. A child is born with its understanding only recently fully linked to its higher conscious self beyond the veil. As it grows, it learns through 3D experience a new set of beliefs and values — the limited, 3D, ego-based, consensus picture. It then experiences the loss of its natural set of non-limiting beliefs that it was born with, in order to enable the growth of the new self-limiting set. Little wonder babies sometimes cry for no apparent reason! Similarly, when the person gets older they can feel that, upon reflection, the set of beliefs by which they had lived was not a source of fulfilment, and so they begin to relinquish them — their teeth begin to fall out.

There is a reason that one person retains healthy, strong teeth to a ripe old age, though their neighbour loses them prematurely. It is a sign that the beliefs they have maintained about life bring them relative contentment and harmony.

If you don't like what you see as your reality, it is imperative that you begin to discipline yourself to start changing what you believe and think. Start exploring new beliefs until you find ones that feel more appropriate for you; beliefs that seem to point towards greater fulfilment, love and harmony.

As long as you continue to believe your reality can only be the way it has always been, or the way it appears now, then you think of it that way and energise it to continue. As soon as you redirect your attention to thoughts and images you find fulfilling, then that will begin to manifest as a more and more fulfilling and real experience for you. Furthermore, as soon as you remove your own beliefs from the collective belief, then the present collective reality is weaker and less able to be sustained. Then you help the world, as the change you have chosen to make will begin to pull the collective reality your way; gradually at first but more strongly as you persist.

All-That-Is always maintains cosmic balance, so every time you take a neutral, allowing, centred stance, accepting that life just is, then the extremes of polarity consciousness will dissolve into harmony. If you allow everything to just be part of all that is potential, leaning to neither polarity and instead embracing it all as just the natural flow of life, it will 'de-polarise'; that is, come into balance and manifest harmoniously as a result. But whenever you take a stand at either end of the polarity scale, the other end must and will manifest to maintain the balance. So if you judge and hold anything as 'good' or 'better', its 'bad' or 'worse' polarity will manifest in your world as a result of your desires. All you need do is see your entire life in that light.

Peace is the experience of a harmonious relationship with all that is in your life. It is gained from letting go of the need to change anything outside of yourself. Seeing the synchronicity in things is a joy in itself. It is making joyous discoveries unexpectedly. The realisation and observation of divine synchronicity gives every moment in life a fresh quality of joy and amusement. It broadens long faces and elevates deep depressions, making life entertaining and full of interest — and meaning. Consequently, the ego is less inclined to run about filling life with trivial attention-seeking and shallow, banal, commercial entertainment that is pumped out to distract us from our truth. Life becomes calm and peaceful. And in profound stillness, the exquisite music of life can be heard on every breeze, and the song of one's inner voice becomes louder and clearer.

Your life is a perfect physical picture of your non-physical consciousness. With that as both a foundation and a motivation, you can build the self-discipline and courage to turn away from the consensus reality (the picture of life that is generally believed to be real) at every instant that you find it less than totally satisfying, in favour of energising and maintaining thought forms of your fulfilment

It is all a matter of choice, and every time you remember you have free will to choose what you experience, you are no longer supporting or feeding your ego's polarity consciousness — your victim mentality and sense of helplessness. You swing to your soul's unity-conscious understanding which originates from beyond the limited physical sphere. You invite in the higher realms of knowing from which your entire reality is nourished with unconditional love, understanding that it will manifest as your experience.

As more people courageously maintain higher and higher states of consciousness, see in each synchronistic moment the truth of their reality through consciously open eyes, and make all choices consciously, then the reality will evolve into a stronger and stronger manifestation of abundance, harmony, joy, freedom, peace and love. Not just for some, but for everybody.

This is happening more and more all over our planet right now. Watch for the synchronicity — 'I was just thinking of that the other day!', 'How amazing, I've been thinking about how I would like one of those!', 'We were just talking about that a moment ago!', 'I was thinking of you and now here you are!', 'You must have read my mind!'

You can stand back and watch, or you can consciously participate, becoming an integral part of a totally new and fulfilling world.

It may not seem easy or comfortable at first because it is habit-breaking in so many ways. But it is very simple. What's more, it is indescribably rewarding and uplifting to experience the transition from the old reality to the new one. It is a big shift from the doldrums of helplessness and hopelessness to joy, abundance, creativity and true power.

The more you listen to your inner voice's unwavering understanding that life is a perfect process of creation offering unlimited choice in beauty, love, fulfilment and harmony, then the more that will become your experience.

The degree to which you listen and bow to your ego's insecure belief in the power of control, dominance and predictability is the degree to which you will experience situations where you feel powerless, attacked or insecure.

It is your choice. Always acknowledge that you are choosing what you are experiencing, then make every choice consciously, rather than unconsciously.

Let nobody convince you that you do not have choice.

Victims transform into potent creators in this way. Their fear of being powerless over circumstances and their loss of hope turns into an ever-increasing sense of purpose, mastery of life, and true power.

Chapter 6

▲

POWER

We all have true power and, unlike control and manipulation, true power is reclaimed through love and allowance, taking responsibility for our own life, thinking with self-discipline, choosing with discernment, and acting with integrity. Fulfilment will then just fall into place automatically. This is how every single person (the meek) shall reclaim their true power and create the life that serves their own highest fulfilment (shall inherit the Earth).

True power does not promote, endorse or support powerlessness in others. Nor is it dominant, controlling, manipulative or overbearing. True power only ever creates an increasing sense of self-esteem, freedom, purpose and sheer love of the unfettered exploration, acceptance and expression of self, along with ever-increasing passion for the unfolding dance of life.

Our true power is reclaimed immediately that we acknowledge responsibility for creating our own reality. Taking absolute responsibility for the creation of our own world of experience opens the door to absolute freedom and our divine purpose in life. That door opens as this principle gives rise to a basic evolutionary realisation: 'I have created this, so I can create anything else if I so choose. Furthermore, I need not and cannot rely on, or wait for, someone else to help or to do it for me. I am not a victim of my circumstances, I am the creator of them. My outer world follows, not leads me.'

Therein lies our ticket to absolute freedom and command over our own lives.

On first engaging this concept, it can seem quite alien to most, a daunting prospect for many, and a ridiculous accusation for some. Such responses are not without reason. After all, the whole of humanity has spent aeons in the habit of giving away, denying and avoiding this true power. We have given our power in various ways to our peers, friends and parents; to representatives of success and of God; to perpetrators of the judgement of right and wrong; to the structured systems of government, religion, culture, economy, education, medicine and science; in fact, to whomever would take care of it for us. We gave our power to anyone and everyone who promised to take responsibility for maintaining our well-being, for relieving our woes and insecurities, and for providing a safe and predictable future for us.

As a result, those we empowered with this responsibility seemed to become our masters, deciding and providing for us. They appeared to have absolute control and we believed we had no power at all over our circumstances. With a vast majority of people supporting this 'mass victim' mentality, humankind's collective consciousness consolidated in polarity and ego, creating a 'mass victim' reality. Fear took over and became the currency of power. We directed our attention — our will and energy to create — into beliefs, thought-forms and images that were given to us, rather than honouring those that originated within us from our ever-loving higher selves. Through increasingly effective mass broadcast, all of our own thoughts and attention — a creative force of daunting potency — were focused onto images of someone else's choice, through a belief system that was inherited, not natural.

However, although we had forgotten about and denied our true power as creators, it had not gone away. We had just redirected it towards the fear, control and victim images to which we were perpetually exposed. We carried on creating, but it only perpetuated and reinforced the *status quo*. As unsatisfactory as it was, humankind's collective reality manifested as physical evidence of the creation process, though we didn't recognise it as such. In itself, this was a reflection of both our perpetual divine power as creators and of our increasingly fear-based polarity consciousness. The guidance couldn't have been clearer, had we remembered our power. But we became like shoals of fish, ducking and diving in unison, reacting to images of the prevailing state of affairs. We turned every-which-way at the whim of someone else's say-so and information, regardless of its basis or intent. Just as long as they'd save us from the things we didn't want to experience.

But at least when something went wrong, there was always someone to blame — not us. Right?

Wrong!

Blame is a victim's view of responsibility. It is a clear

sign of a person in fear of their circumstances, and of their spiritual responsibility to discipline their scattered thoughts and harness their own true power.

Rather than taking responsibility for our own beliefs and actions, we had let others tell us what was right and wrong, good and bad, acceptable and unacceptable, safe and unsafe — even what was true and false. In believing we were victims of our circumstances, we thought that fulfilment, too, would come from outside ourselves. We had given up our own will and ability to discern in our heart of hearts what was truly appropriate. We had given up hearing and trusting our own inner voice from our higher consciousness, even though it is only ever intent on us being ecstatically fulfilled in every conceivable way, dare we listen to its loving whisper. In turning away from our divine guidance, we had also given up the courage to act upon our own truth, instead allowing ourselves to be told by others, and to be punished by them if we didn't agree or behave within their dictated guidelines.

In essence, we gave up believing in ourselves.

This could appear to be a profound lesson in fear, control and irresponsibility; or maybe a sad, even hopeless manifestation of self-denial. Regardless, it is astonishing to think what powerful master-creators we truly are and have always been, given any thought form on which to focus our attention.

But rectifying the entire situation is simple: astonishingly simple.

All we need do is remember our true power — our mastery of creation. To nourish the seed-memory that has always been within us — that of free will and unlimited creative dominion. This seed's nourishment is self-love — allowing ourselves to acknowledge that true self; practising being that unique and potent creative force; accepting and exercising absolute responsibility for it; and learning to consciously live and work with it in every moment.

Thus, every single one of us will be instantaneously empowered. Such power and responsibility can be daunting at first, but take heart. It sets us free from everything and everyone that has ever held us in self-limiting beliefs — the ones (including our own egos) that keep telling us that we're not good enough, wrong, bad, lacking, vulnerable, hopeless and powerless. It also instantly sets about dissolving experiences of pain, struggle, discontent and conflict within and around us. It turns us into glowing beacons in the darkest days of our third-dimensional reality.

This is how everyone will reclaim their own personal power, a power that is as great as Divine Omnipotence itself, because it is God — the unlimited, omnipresent, omnipotent energy of All-That-Is pouring through each and every one of us, creating life constantly just for the experience of it.

It is crucial to remember that this process of turning feelings of helplessness and vulnerability into feelings of confidence and power is achieved through experience, not through theory — through being it, not just knowing or thinking about it.

If you are to change your powerlessness into

empowerment, you must get out of your head and into heartfelt action. You must ground your own higher consciousness and understanding into your physical world, like earthing a gargantuan power generator. You will do this by *being* its truths — by living them, not just expounding them.

Only when you are experiencing what it feels like in action have you allowed your own truth out of your head, through your heart and into your reality. Only then are you evolving by living your spiritual purpose — by sharing your own inner wisdom in this density; by being your own unique manifestation of love and truth in the earthly realm. Until then, you have resisted your higher self, your own divinity and the flow of creation through you, living your fear and polarity illusion instead.

When you have a totally joyous and fulfilling reality in every single respect, then you can thank yourself — not anyone or anything else — for your wisdom, self-love, discernment, courage, integrity and spiritual diligence. But if you feel the slightest need to defend or compromise yourself, or someone else, your sense of joy and fulfilment, your beliefs or your circumstances in any way, then you are still in fear and polarity consciousness.

When you choose, you can create something more loving and harmonious in any instant. First, accept what is, and look at your existing feelings and attitudes towards it as one option. Next, expand your thinking to include other options; ones that would be more in keeping with your own truth about a joyous, loving and fulfilled you. Then turn your attention to only the option most faithful to your deepest truth and sense of joy and fulfilment, choosing to focus on no other.

If you do so and life seems no different, then your beliefs and thoughts have not truly changed either. Alternatively, they haven't had time to consolidate into a new belief system that you hold as your truth. By redirecting every memory and every moment to the self-loving truthful option, old experiences will not be energised as thought-forms and will not be able to exist as they were.

With adherence through self-love, self-discipline and integrity, new experiences of more fulfilling quality will increasingly transmute the old ones or overtake them.

The new manifestations will be examples of continually evolving beliefs, not the ultimate ones, and it will serve you to read them as such. They are perfect examples of your ability to create, as they are perfectly accurate reflections of the beliefs and thoughts that you are presently giving the most attention. That is their inherent beauty and perfection. Anything else is your ego's judgement of their quality.

All experience is absolutely neutral creation until the instant ego judges it. Only then does it appear to be good or bad, right or wrong, desirable or undesirable. Only then does it represent anything other than divine perfection, and even then only to the ego concerned. At that instant, it turns into a valuable measure of the degree to which fear still has a grip, how far one is removed from their spiritual truth and mission in life, and how deeply they are still immersed in the old patterning of third dimensional, self-limiting, polarity consciousness.

This system sets up a new path of empowerment, not an instantaneous result. It is simply a flow to which self-discipline may be applied, and which brings about new sensations and experiences in life. The manifestations will become increasingly fulfilling to the extent that one can embrace and uphold their new beliefs and thoughts, and ignore the old influences that may still be around them.

> Being in love-based, high-frequency consciousness (unity-consciousness), I allow everything to just be, remembering and thinking of only the things that make me feel more joyous. I feed only those thought-forms energy by putting my attention only on them, and they become my experience. This manifests as quickly and as accurately as I choose to allow the energy of higher understanding to flow and love to express through me. I therefore let go of any resistance as it symbolises my resistance to life itself, and therefore to the life force which is the very energy of which all things in my entire reality are formed.

This is a statement of intent: a stream of new belief. It is a new undercurrent of energy in a new direction, flavouring everything you think, say and do — everything you are experiencing and being. Everything you are.

To enact this requires courage and self-love.

Chapter 7

▲

LOVE

The moment of accepting self in every detail without hesitation is the moment your life begins to turn into love and out of fear. It is the passport to empowerment and to the soul's unity consciousness from ego's polarity consciousness. Above all, it instantly begins the most meaningful healing process, enabling the flow of all of the perfect guidance and harmony that love holds in store.

Love is just letting everything be, whatever it is and however it seems to be. It is not as trite as needing or liking something a whole lot more than anything else — those are attributes of ego's desire-oriented fearful viewpoint.

Think of love as allowance. When you allow yourself to be who you are, without any hesitation or conditions, then you are in unconditional love — divine love. From this viewpoint, you can see yourself differently. You are able to see the falseness of all guilt, judgement, self-denial, criticism and resistance you might have ever held for yourself in your life. You can see your true essence — your divine purity. You can see that anything you have ever thought about your own imperfections has just been a misunderstanding. You are, and always have been, absolutely perfectly yourself at every moment to get you to where you are now, experiencing what you had chosen to experience. This has all been your own individual contribution to complete the wholeness of All-That-Is. When you choose to see it all without judgement, to allow it all to be perfect, then you'll realise it is.

Perfection is not good, and it is not a destination. It is simply the fact that everything in every moment is ideal to maintain balance in the cosmos. Therefore you are always in the perfect place, at the perfect time, in the perfect way. You don't need to justify yourself, like or dislike yourself — just allow yourself to be. You only need to love yourself without any hesitation, conditions or compromises whatsoever. When you allow yourself to see the inherent perfection of everything now, then you are in harmony. Only on the calmness of your inner ocean of peace can you see the reflection of yourself clearly. Only then can you hear your inner voice and accurately assess what serves your highest truth in the moment.

You may change yourself if you wish to embrace something else that feels more in tune with you, and as a result, what you experience will change in order to maintain cosmic balance. As you come into harmony with what is now, then it will come into harmony with you or it will dissolve away. Either way, you will maintain clarity and peace and thereby add to the peacefulness of your world. You will be loving your life.

When you observe and honour yourself in this way, you can honestly decide whether or not you are being true to your self by assessing whether or not your life is increasingly fulfilling and joyous. If it is, then you are on your path, living your higher purpose. If it is not, then from this standpoint of truth, you have a stable base from which to evaluate, make changes, build and evolve. You can start experiencing a different reality by being different to the way you were. As you think lovingly, with allowance, your mirror-world will begin to reflect it to you more and more as loving experience. If you wish, you can also change it again in the next instant, and again and again. Only you are stopping or allowing your progress to greater joy and fulfilment. You are unlimited in your potential to pursue the experience of joy, love, abundance and fulfilment — in our third-dimensional reality or in any other.

Now, the biggest change will quite possibly creep up on you. As you allow yourself to be absolutely who you are at every instant, using each experience as a platform to observe your self-love, you begin to see everyone and everything outside of you in exactly the same light of unity consciousness. You unconditionally allow others to be themselves, your compassion blossoming in the understanding that they are not only doing whatever they came to do, but they are a part of you that you observe as your reflection, and *vice versa*. Their being themselves is their divine gift to you, as is your being yourself, the gift to them. In that light you can be of compassionate service and support to them, assisting them in coming into love with themselves also.

The degree to which you love yourself uncon-ditionally is the only degree to which you can truly be of service to another. Outside of that you will only be projecting your conditional biases onto them, making it even more difficult for them to find and honour their own divinity.

Unconditional love, like perfection, is not good, neither is it a destination. Unconditional love is a way of living, a continuing journey. It is a path of constant allowance of what you are and what is at every instant, lock, stock and barrel. That negates the pressure or desire to change anything outside yourself.

Unconditional self-love asks you to allow yourself to be, and to evaluate each moment and experience in terms of your own true joy and fulfilment. It calls for conscious self-discipline to allow the truth in each moment to become known, even if it is simply that the prevailing situation is perfect manifestation. It also asks you to maintain thoughts and beliefs of fulfilment so that they will continue to become your experience more comprehensively. This is your own responsibility, and no other can do it for you.

Every single person can plant this seed just by choosing to do so. Remember that to love someone or something, even a situation, does not mean needing to like it, but rather just allowing it to be. This gives us the freedom to choose how we might respond to it. Also, it allows the birth of truth in our living reality.

Truth is subjective. Everyone has their very own, which is perfect for them. It is what they sense most strongly right now to be true for them — what 'rings' true. Therefore, the voice of truth can only originate from within. In this way, truth puts the horse in front of the cart once more, acknowledging that what is outside of us follows, not leads us.

Allowing everything and everyone to just *be* may at first sound like blindly accepting it all as your own truth, but that is not so. It is necessary to allow everything if you are to become at peace and live in harmony with all creation. However, it is not required that you indiscriminately accept it, as though it is automatically of service to you personally, or for your ultimate fulfilment. Neither is it required that you put your energy into it to make it part of your own reality. What anyone else chooses is their business, and you love them for honouring their truth, which you must assume they are doing since they are the only one able to hear their inner voice. Life presents an infinite spectrum of possibilities from which anyone may choose. To find your own truth in amongst it all and to identify what you choose to energise as your own experience requires discernment.

Discernment is listening to your heart. It is attunement to the inner voice of your soul which knows and understands all, not to your ego, which wishes it did so that it could get control. It enables you to feel what is true to you for your greatest fulfilment, highest expression and experience of love. Discernment asks you to look at what will nurture the joy in you and what will enhance your sense of self-worth and true power, not your vanity and control. It enables you to get a clearer picture of what encourages and supports your sense of freedom and love, not limitation and fear. It allows your deep inner knowing to be your guide, rather than external experience or opinion.

The answers and realisations that arise through listening to your own inner voice may feel uncomfortable or unfamiliar at first, but they give you choice. With choice, you are free. Without choice, you feel trapped and a victim once more.

Conscious thoughts about what is outside of you are constantly clouded by outside influences. When you take time to quieten the thoughts from your conscious mind, you become more and more proficient at hearing the quiet strength of your heartfelt truths. These truths become stronger and clearer as you listen to them. The heart is allowing, not controlling. It enables you to see a wider horizon of choices; choices which lie outside the present streams of expectation and influence to which your ego limits you.

Discernment is the ideal filter for every thought and circumstance. Is what you are thinking about what you truly want? Or is it about what you don't want? After all, it will manifest as your experience, regardless. Is what you are experiencing what you want as part of your ongoing reality, or not? As you sense the inner answers to such questions, trust them as your truth. Live by them without hesitation or compromise — it will heighten your integrity.

Integrity is discernment put into action. It is better to honour that soft inner voice of your higher self at every instant and think you are wrong, than to not listen to yourself. Because 'wrong' is just an ego judgement and an illusion, the chances of going against the will of the Absolute are exceedingly remote. Impossible, I would say. After all, humanity has had aeons of practice at ignoring their inner voices, and our present world — plagued by conflict, hatred, pain, war, disease, sorrow, scarcity and struggle — is the living result of it. It's about time we tried something else — something completely different!

It takes courage to live truth, especially when that truth flies in the face of differing beliefs that others hold. But just because your belief is different, doesn't make it right or wrong, and the next person's the opposite. It just means they are different. Being different offers more choice. It is actually an expression of love, freedom and allowance to have differing beliefs. When someone feels hurt or upset or challenged by a different truth, it is still their choice to feel that way.

None of us can hurt or upset another, nor they us. It is invariably everyone's own choice how they respond to everything.

You must live your truth or you are living a lie. If you were to compromise your truth by living to satisfy or placate outside influences or to pussy-foot around someone else's ego, you would be fooling yourself horribly. You would not be living your truth and you would be denying them theirs at the same time. Their ego is not their truth, just as your ego is not yours.

It is your responsibility to hold to your own truth until such time as you choose to modify it to encompass even more love, joy, abundance and contentment.

It is their responsibility to do the same.

Chapter 8

▲

RESPONSIBILITY

You are the only one responsible for you. If another takes responsibility for you, you lose both freedom and power, as does anyone for whom you take responsibility. Every action you take is your choice and you are always responsible for it. Your past choices and actions have brought you to where you are right now, and you are responsible for maintaining or changing it.

Responsibility is the ability to respond. To respond is to experience life's circumstances in a loving and allowing way, coming from the irrepressible spiritual knowledge of your own divine power to create and choose at will, fully aware of your present truths and understandings of yourself and all that is, and with the integrity and courage to put them into action in every moment — to actually live them.

To react, on the other hand, is to experience life's circumstances in a fearful, resistant and controlling way, according to the ego's polarity consciousness beliefs that you are not in command of your life, that you are a victim of circumstance and are therefore powerless to do anything except complain or blame the perpetrators of your predicament.

The big difference between these is your choice to be in your power or not to be. The choice to acknowledge your role as creator is your ultimate spiritual responsibility — to be centred in yourself and in your divine purpose. The sooner you take your power and take responsibility for it, the sooner you will have it to wield at will; and the sooner you will be free.

Part of responsibility includes recognising others' responsibility as being equally significant and empowering for them. Remove the plank from your own eye before trying to remove the splinter from another's. It will serve us well to remember not to try to take responsibility for another's life or creations, regardless of who they are or what their experience looks like to us. As soon as we apply our values to another's experience, we create all manner of new control and ego issues for ourselves and for them to stumble through. Disharmony is always the result.

First, our ego is judging that what they are experiencing is not right or appropriate for them; not safe or desirable; not for their highest good. But, contrary to our ego beliefs, we are not capable of evaluating these things. Nobody is but the person concerned.

Second, our ego is trying to control them into doing what we judge to be right or good for them or someone else. In such ways we are actually giving them another opportunity to give away their power — to us — by giving away their responsibility to listen to their own inner voice. We disable their discernment and dissolve their divine right to choose and create for themselves —

to be free. We are keeping them from fulfilment, not leading them to it!

Third, it is promoting fear in them that what they are doing is not right and that they will be judged on it. Their fear will only inflame their ego and its fear-based manifestations, adding to everybody's experience of a polarity-conscious world. After all, we are not separate in the infinite ocean of consciousness that's all that is, so it will only slow both us and them down.

As soon as we respond to others with unconditional love, allowing them to be exactly who they are choosing to be without judgement, everything can begin to heal — to come into alignment with truth and harmony. This requires the courage to respond to them in our own truth and with integrity, not in avoidance, disallowance, resistance, judgement or control. Simultaneously, we give them the choice and opportunity to do the same without our ego reacting to them.

Only then are we responsible in a truly spiritual sense and acting in true service. True service is maintaining your own highest vibration while assisting others to maintain theirs. It requires being unconditionally loving of ourselves and of others, taking responsibility for our power and giving others responsibility for theirs, whatever they choose to do with it.

Imagine you are feeling on top of the world and getting comfortable astride your new-found unity-consciousness belief system (high-frequency energy). A friend or loved one calls or meets you. They are feeling horribly depressed (low-frequency energy). Because the entire cosmos maintains perfect balance permanently, it naturally tends towards harmony. Disharmony is simply imbalance in energy frequencies. This is what is commonly referred to as being 'on a different wavelength'. So in the instance of the depressed friend, a number of different things could happen in order to bring your differing frequencies out of conflict to maintain harmony.

On one hand, you could pity them and come down into their depression (lower your frequency by agreeing with their sad circumstances, feeling sorry for them, or complaining with them about outside influences). But that is not of service.

Alternatively, you could find that you can't stand their state (the frequency of their present consciousness) and cut contact to preserve your peace of mind (in which case you may be doing resistance and setting up other energy-challenging fear and control issues for yourself). However, you could find yourself unable to escape them for some reason and, not wanting to be depressed like them, groping for a unity-consciousness approach that is aligned with love, allowance, discernment and integrity.

The most spiritually responsible solution is to first understand that you had manifested the situation for a higher reason and that from it you have the power to create something else of higher fulfilment for both. It is crucial to your integrity that you honour the most fulfilling and joyous state. Therefore, to fall within their depression is not of service to them nor to you. Have the courage to maintain your state of high energy by remaining in your joy. Be amused at the amazing way you'd both manifested such a polarity for yourselves — why would you have created that? What is it reflecting to you? Be happy that they are living their own perfect manifestations as well. Don't judge it as good or bad, or you will become trapped in the ego's need to 'fix' them or their situation to make it suit your truth.

When you stand in your frequency in this way, two important things happen. First, you'll see the truth more clearly and easily from your detached position, and you'll be able to be of true service. Second, the problem will disappear because they will either come out of their depression (come up nearer to your frequency) or they'll leave your space because they can't stand you being happy in their presence.

But by having the courage and integrity to be your own energy (that is, maintain your own vibration), you've given them a choice — to be depressed or be happy. Being depressed is the opposite of their highest expression so you are also doing them a favour in being a reminder for them, whether they realise it or not. You are being both of service to them and self-loving by allowing yourself to be in your own highest expression. What's more, you'll have risen to the challenge of the opportunity you'd created for yourself to honour your unity-consciousness and to be of service to another soul who'd forgotten theirs.

This may not be the way you have learned to deal with such a situation, but that does not make it inappropriate, just new and different. Perpetuating the old mentality perpetuates the old reality. Whether they know or can accept these things in their existing mindset or not, does not alter the truth of the matter. It does, however, give you the opportunity to express it to them lovingly, compassionately and unconditionally, if and when the situation provides.

True compassion and caring are not feel-good quick-fixes. They require your uncompromised inner truth as their base, or you will only be using them in fearful or emotionally controlling ways. Sometimes, true compassion and care will not make a person feel good initially, but they will heal. Anyway, what kind of loving friend or healer would lie to you so that you'd feel good in the interim, only to face it all again later? Only one who would be avoiding themselves feeling uncomfortable with the truth in the circumstances. And that would be fear, the opposite of love.

If you give help where it is not asked, remember you are then doing control and expectation which is polarity consciousness, ego-based, judgemental and fearful. On the other hand, if you were to *offer* help, you give them choice which is unity-consciousness and a compassionate expression of love. If they do not accept your offers and you feel either hurt or happy, unwanted or relieved, then you are in your ego again. If, on the other hand, you feel neutral, then you are being loving, detached and allowing of their truth at the time. If they accept and you feel anything but neutral, you are in ego as well.

Disciplining your own attitudes to keep you on the path of fruitful evolvement is your own responsibility, and an expression of self-love.

Any form of discipline of anyone or anything outside of yourself is control, based on your ego's expectation or judgement of good or bad, right or wrong. It is not love, it is fear. There are no exceptions. It is also destructive to higher consciousness since it is compromising spiritual responsibility.

Since all of your beliefs and thoughts manifest for you, it is your responsibility to discipline what your mind is focused upon. With a little thought, you will find very simple but effective ways to apply this in your day-to-day life. One such way is to choose to stop buying and reading newspapers and watching television. They constantly infect human minds' potential for self-generated thought — creative thought. This infection is the plethora of fear-based images — conflict, drama, pain, scarcity, disappointment and struggle, on physical, emotional and mental levels. As you allow your mind to be directed to them, they are empowered to be the continuing reality. That is how individuals personally contribute to the state of the world. Such potent images overwhelm your ability to think for yourself, filling your consciousness with negativity.

If you are happy with what you see of the world, then fine. If not, then stop the flow of those images into your mind by turning off the television and ignoring the newspapers. Immediately, you'll be able to generate more loving and fulfilling thought-forms in their place. And they'll begin to manifest instead of the present reality.

As we come to understand through experience the finer points of the flow of energy throughout our life, we learn to manage our own energy with increasing love and allowance. In doing so, we come into still higher-frequency consciousness and become more and more directly aligned with our soul, our higher self and our true spiritual mission in the dimension of physical embodiment. As this comes about we are healing ourselves, humankind and our experiential playground — planet Earth.

Chapter 9

▲

HEALING

You can't heal anyone but yourself, and nobody else can heal you. Healing is more than getting rid of symptoms in your body. It is acknowledging their origin and purpose, and lovingly releasing fear and discord from your mental, emotional and physical vibrations so that the symptoms are no longer required. Physical dis-ease is the last resort your soul has to communicate to you the dis-ease in your consciousness, which you cannot escape, only heal. If you just fix the symptoms, you ignore and crush their divine guidance.

Just as your own belief system creates your outer world, so it creates your personal world. Your body is simply a physical, three-dimensional model of your conscious and subconscious beliefs and thoughts. It is the most accurate model possible since it is a collection of so many malleable parts, each of which is a perfect reflection of its corresponding part in your belief system.

The body is an infallible messaging system from the soul to a person's present conscious personality regarding where they are out of harmony with themselves and all that is in the flow of creation.

The human being is a single field or ball of energy, vibrating in a vast spectrum of frequencies. You could say that this energy field is divided into two parts, though they are only divided in our physical-world view. They are the physical part (body) and the non-physical part (aura, or subtle energy field) which surrounds and permeates it. These parts exist simultaneously and interact constantly. They only appear to be different because of the different spectrum of vibrations each maintains. The physical body is a set of low enough frequencies to maintain material density, and the rest is high enough frequency to exist in the intangible range of frequencies beyond plain eyesight. Nonetheless, they do exist in vibrations beyond our visible spectrum, just like microwaves, ultraviolet and infra-red waves, and the auras of all living things (Figure 9.1).

Figure 9.1

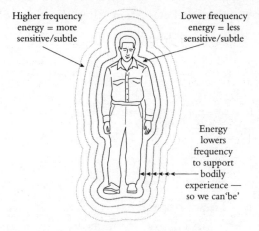

Higher frequency energy = more sensitive/subtle

Lower frequency energy = less sensitive/subtle

Energy lowers frequency to support bodily experience — so we can 'be'

Being beyond physical vibrations, the auric body (subtle energy field) contains all of the non-physical higher energies of thought and emotion. These produce corresponding symptoms in the material body.

There is nothing 'wrong' with symptoms. Again, they are simply reflections — signals of the dis-eased, polarity and fear-based beliefs and thoughts to which one gives the most attention. If you do not recognise your own fear, resistance or disallowance at the subtler levels of thoughts, attitudes and emotions and go about consciously bringing them into harmony, they gradually become physical symptoms. When the thoughts and emotions are loving and harmonious, the physical body will display symptoms of harmony and well-being; if they are disharmonious, the body will display symptoms of pain and dis-ease.

In the human consciousness this flow is *through* your underlying beliefs, not *from* them. Our own consciousness and its acquired belief system filter the flow of divine energy into our physical realm, beginning with the thought, connecting with the physical body through the emotions, then appearing in the physical world as a bodily symptom. Examples of this 'thought/emotion/physical symptom' flow are 'self-doubt/embarrassment/hot flush'; 'approval/happiness/smile'; 'loss/sorrow/weeping'.

The higher vibrational auric body is where one initially experiences the effects of resistance and allowance. These respectively congest or liberate the natural flow of energy throughout the non-physical bodies. Non-physical mental and emotional symptoms subsequently manifest in the subtle energy field, or aura, which then becomes a mixture of blocked, congested or 'crystallised' energies, and smoothly flowing ones. Blocks are maintained as one perpetuates beliefs in the need to resist feelings and sensations, thoughts and beliefs, and other phenomena. When this happens, the vibration of the energy continues to get lower and lower in frequency until it drops into the physical spectrum and physical symptoms begin to appear.

The physical body is simply a collection of symptoms reflecting conscious and unconscious beliefs in the need to resist the flow of feelings, sensations, thoughts and life experience. Remember, these symptoms are just signals created to alert the body's owner to the mortal effects of denying one's life purpose and divinity by controlling and resisting the natural flow of life. They are only physical because the preceding non-physical ones were consistently ignored. When read like the signals on the instrument panel of a car, they describe the state of a person's acceptance of self, their tendency to control or allow, and the resistance they have to the natural flow of life — higher truth, unconditional love and allowance in the physical experiential world. As one becomes further removed from their highest expression (their spiritual mission; their divinity and life purpose) and less at ease with the truth of who they are, the symptoms become increasingly numerous, uncomfortable and difficult to ignore. The person consequently experiences dis-ease.

As individuals come into contact and harmony with their souls' truth-expression, they feel at ease with themselves, allowing themselves to just be who they truly are. That is to say, they love themselves unconditionally and accept responsibility for themselves and their own life. As this self-awareness comes to flourish, their mental, emotional and physical activity come to reflect it and their physical symptoms become less noticeable since the person is in harmony with themselves. They experience wellness as a result.

It is important to realise that healing does not mean getting rid of symptoms that one finds uncomfortable. That is an automatic by-product of healing.

Healing is raising the vibration of energy (consciousness) so that symptoms of dis-ease (self limitation) can no longer continue to exist or manifest in the body. Thus, we find that one of the ways higher consciousness manifests is in a less dis-eased body. Healing is bringing your entire belief system into harmony with your higher consciousness. It is allowing the soul's divine understanding to merge with the ego's polarised mis-perceptions so that truth can prevail and be experienced in actions. This enables one to remember and live the truth that you are more than a victim in a physical body wandering this planet needing to be protected. You are a divine spirit, living and creating through a physical body whose natural state is perpetually perfect form and function at any given instant.

In short, to heal, one must allow unconditional love in, as well as express it outwardly where fear, resistance and control had prevailed.

It also carries the big tag of responsibility, because nobody can do another's healing. Even if they try to and succeed, the person who is subject to the healing is also subject to a change in their consciousness and in their life experience accordingly. They may not be ready for that, and nobody but they are able to know or are qualified to decide. Anyone who thinks another person needs healing is being judgemental and in polarity consciousness — judging that the person's health or situation is bad, wrong, inappropriate or unacceptable. But even in pain, there are those who don't want or are not ready to let it go, and that's their choice.

If someone is in deep mourning over losing a loved one, who are we to decide that their sorrow is not right for them? Who are we to try and make them feel better, taking from them the experience of such a profound connection with the departed person? We would basically be telling them that we have decided their feelings are not appropriate or good for them and we are going to take them away. Would that promote less choice or more? Is it loving and allowing? No, it's fearful and controlling. It is ego inflicting subjective judgements on someone else's life and state of being.

If they invite help, directly or indirectly, then that is an entirely different matter because they have begun to take responsibility. You can then give them choice by responding, remembering to do so unconditionally, in your own truth, without any expectation of the type of response you might get, and remaining unattached to whatever result you might achieve. Then, and only then, can the healer function.

Healers simply provide an opportunity and a means

for a person to heal. They are conduits through which energy pours, exposing manifestations of lower vibrational energy (lower consciousness) to the flow of higher vibrational energy (higher consciousness). This dissolves the fearful and resistant mental and emotional patterning in the subject's energy field which is manifesting as symptoms. It is like a block of ice being raised in vibration until it dissolves into steam. The disparate frequencies of the healing energy and the subject's come into balance through the process of osmosis, and either the healer's vibration falls lower or the subject's rises higher.

There lies every healer's responsibility and a vital focal point for their true service and integrity, and for anyone else's for that matter. It is of no service to weep the tears of another nor take on their pains or emotions. It is spiritually irresponsible in that it reinforces the lower-consciousness aspects of both healer and subject. After all, healing cannot become complete on a permanent basis without the subject altering their thoughts and beliefs that brought about the symptoms. Many dis-eases continue to plague humankind, recurring because the people have not altered their beliefs about life and themselves, all of which are the basis of all their thoughts, attitudes and emotions.

Healing undermines the ability of physical dis-ease to exist by addressing the underlying belief systems on an energetic level, rather than the gross physical one. In that way, it suffocates the symptoms, disabling them from continuing to manifest. That is how any person can take responsibility for their own well-being and participate in their own healing by assisting any healer who works with them.

It is critically important to remember that one does not need to be ill to benefit from healing. When the symptoms have fallen to the physical level, they have become deeply ingrained over time and generally require more time and energy work to dissolve. It is much more efficient to perform healing on the non-physical level. There, the changes can happen more rapidly because the energy is at a much higher vibration and therefore more malleable. Any dis-ease in the energy field which is on course to manifest physically is dissolved before it can do so. Maintaining harmony in our subtler energy field of beliefs, thoughts, attitudes and emotions is of higher consciousness than waiting to keep harmony in the material body once the symptoms manifest themselves physically. That raises another important point: the best healer any of us can ever have is ourselves.

When we detect the problem in our consciousness, discern its origin in our beliefs, redirect our thoughts and attitudes with unconditional love accordingly, and live that truth with integrity and courage, we will heal automatically. Also, we will have addressed our basic consciousness issues more deeply and thoroughly across the board. This is due to the very process of self-re-evaluation, and the self-loving act of consciously caring about and taking responsibility for our own well-being.

Alternatively, there are many types of subtle healing

that have come into our awareness and experience over recent times. That these healing modalities continue to arise is a sign that the collective consciousness is raising and releasing higher vibrational understanding into our physical world. These subtle healing modalities are all spiritual healing of a type. They include auric healing, hands-on healing, naturopathy, colour healing, homeopathy, crystal healing, flower essences, naturally-energised waters and oils, kinesiology, herbal therapy, vocal and instrumental sonic healing, acupuncture, spiritual counselling, body work such as massage and pulsing, and the many variations of each.

Such healing systems work with the flow of energy in the subtle energy field, enabling it to flow more naturally and easily through avenues in our physical and auric bodies called meridians. Our meridians make sure our entire energy field is energised correctly. They facilitate the natural flow of life force from our higher consciousness into this physical, third-dimensional experience we are having. They become blocked or congested by resistant thoughts and attitudes stemming from our ego's polarity-conscious fear beliefs. The more they are blocked, the less easily life flows and the more we are plagued with dis-ease symptoms.

We can live three weeks without food, three days without water and three minutes without air.

We stop living the instant that life force stops flowing through us.

Chapter 10

▲

LIFE FORCE

Throughout the ages, various cultures around the world have used different terms to identify the same fundamental energy. They include prana, chi, kundalini, ki, neuma, orgone, mana, spirit, life energy and divine energy. By any name, it is the life force; the eternal fuel of being — life itself. It flows through us, not to us, enabling us to live and love, create and experience, feel and grow.

We can choose to allow life to flow, or we can choose to block it. The blocks are our ego's resistance to the natural flow of life, believing it needs control if it is going to experience safety and fulfilment physically, emotionally and mentally. But the less life force that flows, the less life we experience. Absolute resistance equals an absolute block — zero flow. That is the experience of zero life. Zero life is death; the relinquishment of the ego-physical, embodied self. Death is actually only the manifestation of our own ego-conscious fear and control taken to its ultimate conclusion.

We are all natural conduits, or channels, for life force. If we were not then we simply could not experience life. Spiritually speaking, the higher self is the channel or passageway through the veil by which All-That-Is connects with our physical reality. It enables our higher consciousness to reach our physical body, feeding it life-force energy constantly. Our physical body thus becomes the channel through which All-That-Is expresses into this universe, creating and experiencing here in its myriad ways. Therefore, the only thing that stops any one of us from functioning consciously as a spiritual master, or a divine being, is our own constrictions which we put upon the life force flowing through us — constrictions determined by our own state of consciousness. Higher consciousness (love, joy and harmony) is more allowing of the life force, whilst lower consciousness (fear and control) is less allowing of it.

This makes each physical body a transducer of consciousness. That is to say, it provides a mechanism by which the vibrational rate of energy can be converted from higher-dimensional consciousness through the veil into our lower, third-dimensional version (Figure 10.1).

Figure 10.1

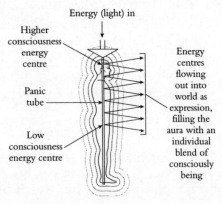

Energy (light) in

Higher consciousness energy centre

Panic tube

Low consciousness energy centre

Energy centres flowing out into world as expression, filling the aura with an individual blend of consciously being

Our higher self allows life-force energy, in the form of pure light, through our non-physical energy field, into our physical body. It does so through a non-physical (etheric) straight passageway resembling a fluorescent tube. Among other things, it is called our I AM Centre, or our pranic tube. This tube then runs vertically down the centre of our physical body from just above the head. It enters through the top of the skull, runs straight down through the head and torso until it exits the body at the perineum near the base of the spine, continuing down to just below the feet. It is actually very precise, with individual dimensions for each person, its diameter being the same as the loop formed by placing together the tips of one's middle finger and thumb. This pranic tube enables the exact maximum flow of life force through the body.

Consciousness, in the form of pure light, enters our head through the tube. It floods and energises the first endocrine gland, the pineal in the centre of the head. Acting like a prism, the pineal gland splits the energy into a spectrum of its constituent frequency bands, rather like a rainbow created from sunlight. This enables us to utilise and experience the life force in a variety of ways through mental, emotional and physical functions. Within the physical body, the spectrum flows into life via a non-physical system of energy exchange centres. They are called chakras in Hindi, meaning 'wheels of fire'. They each function at a different frequency band of the energy and interact with the physical body to enliven it in all ways.

Our physical bodies have seven major energy exchange centres. Each one has both an endocrine gland and major organ/s relating to it in the physical body. Therefore, each also relates to a physical bodily process and hormone function. It also has a colour and sound tone, a fragrance and a taste related to its frequency. This is the basis of many of the subtle energy healing systems.

The vibrational energy of each of our energy exchange centres enables us to experience movement, sensation and thought because of its interaction with our physical self. It allows us our experience of life through expressions made (energy enacted, sent outwards) and impressions gained (energy sensed, received inwards). If we suppress thoughts, feelings or actions, we control and limit the outward flow through one or more of these vital energy centres. When we resist ideas, images, sensations and experiences, we similarly control and limit the inward flow. The energy then becomes blocked and the balance of all the energy centres is upset. This highlights the need for absolute self-love — absolute allowance of all self-expression to maintain balance, harmony and well-being.

Our entire energy exchange centre system strives to maintain delicate balance so that we can experience a full spectrum of life. It steps down the energy vibration like a personal microcosm of the energy stepping down through the higher dimensions of consciousness to reach ours, as described in Chapter 2.

The highest frequency energy centre, the crown, is at the top of the head. It is the seventh and enables us to receive the life-force energy from the higher dimensions. It relates to the pineal gland and the upper brain, primarily affecting mental and nervous activity. Stepping down in frequency and becoming a little more physically oriented, the sixth, between and just above the eyes, is associated with the pituitary gland and lower brain. It deals with inspiration, imagination, ideas and intuition, as well as the senses of hearing, smell and taste. Next is the fifth, situated in the throat. Its endocrine link is with the thyroid gland and its organ is primarily the lungs. It affects bronchial, vocal and alimentary matters, as well as the function of truth and clarity in verbal communication, and grief and remorse. The fourth is the heart centre in the middle of the chest, aligned with the thymus gland and the heart itself. It deals with experiences of love and affection, loyalty and compassion, as well as truth in feelings. Next lower is the third, the solar plexus, relating to the pancreas and the liver and stomach. The activity of digestion and the sensations of anger and control, learning and attitude are its domain. Second to lowest is the sacral centre near the navel. It energises the gonads and affects the reproductive organs, dealing with one's experience of such issues as relationships, sexuality and emotional matters past and present. Lowest is the base centre situated at the perineum near the base of the spine. Linked to the adrenal glands, spinal column and kidneys, it relates to sensations of survival, fear and uncertainty. It enables us to experience and respond to mortal fear during potentially life-threatening situations.

This is a very simple overview of the system, considering these energy exchange centres are also interlinked in subtle ways with each other. However, when this system is in balance — that is, when we are not resisting expressions or impressions — we are in harmony and our mental, emotional and physical health is fine. Our organs are functioning properly, our energies are flowing naturally, and we feel well.

Becoming well is simply a matter of allowing the flow of life to happen unconditionally and without resistance. It is trusting in the knowledge that one's higher self is directing everything and is only interested in us experiencing a reality of love, abundance, fulfilment and self-expression in our physical world. Our body is our personal vehicle for such experience. It is like the chassis of a car which holds together all the vital components so that the complete automobile can serve as transportation. Being so, it is our responsibility to take care of it.

Conventional medical practice and pharmaceuticals are designed to get rid of undesirable symptoms as quickly as possible, whether it's a runny nose or a cancerous tumour. But they are not of creative and loving high consciousness at all; they are third-dimensional, intellectually-driven, control-based belief systems and technologies. Self-interested, resistant to change and fearful of contradiction, they continually inflame and re-infect humanity's victim beliefs. They do so by ignoring and avoiding the true causes of dis-ease symptoms instead of addressing them.

Just like the flat Earth, old beliefs are perpetuated far

beyond usefulness; and like Leonardo da Vinci's helicopter concept, new ideas and attitudes are ignored, resisted and ridiculed without foundation. This is largely the result of control-mongers steering the path of evolution and the dissemination of knowledge, power and freedom.

Humanity's present state of health is the result of such control, as are the companies pumping out a proliferation of unnatural pharmaceutical products and the high degree of investment in medical institutions and technologies. In being painfully slow to acknowledge any alternative explanations, today's medical system has severed itself from deeper understanding of the very things it seeks to cure. It has become an archaic and irrelevant system — the 'flat earth society' of health care. It is holding on fast to systems and beliefs that are being perpetuated through sheer inflexibility and ego-resistance to impending contradiction. It has also proven itself incapable of fulfilling its promise to cure dis-eases such as the common cold and cancer. The reason such ailments rear their ugly heads repeatedly in a person is that, though pharmaceuticals or surgery may remove the symptom, the origin or cause in the dis-eased consciousness is still not addressed. But the annoying warning lights are put out temporarily, so the person doesn't see or sense any need to address them: a fatal mistake.

Remember, energy forms everything, and our body cells are no exception. Like everything else, they are formed according to our beliefs. If our beliefs are basically infected with unnatural and disharmonious influences, so will be our cells, organs and entire body. Even after radical surgery that removes dis-eased cells with a huge safety margin, the uninformed patient often continues creating deformed, infected or dis-eased cells in their body and the symptom returns. And it will continue to do so until the cause is addressed at its source — in their consciousness. In some cases it does not return and this can be for two reasons. First, the person's damaging belief system is not intense enough to compound the problem again before they die of some other cause. Second, the medical treatment or surgery has provided an opportunity for the person to reassess their belief system and change their life accordingly.

Heart disease is a good example of the latter, where a person is often required to find the time to rest and convalesce. During this time such a person often ponders their relationships with the people around them, with life itself and, ultimately, with themselves. They may decide that people, particularly their loved ones, are more important than the stress and worry of other aspects of their life. Their priorities shift and unwittingly they have begun to address the message from their higher consciousness telling them that they were ignoring, suppressing, resisting or conditioning in some way the expressions of love in their life. Imbalance addressed — attitudes and beliefs changed — no more signals needed — heart dis-ease doesn't return. Simple. But if it had been addressed on a subtler level, the drugs and surgery would never have been required.

Through the law of cause-and-effect, our dis-harmonious, dis-eased beliefs and attitudes we hold within ourselves must and will manifest in the corresponding area of our body in due course. In this instance of the heart, let's say the person has a basic belief that to love is to expose oneself to possible emotional trauma, discomfort or even physical danger. This could stem from childhood experiences or high-impact events while growing up. So they go about suppressing and manipulating the multitude of love experiences in their life. Outwardly, this might manifest as a relationship with someone who is unable or unwilling to express their love, or who is distrusting of their partner. It might be somebody who is constantly the 'rescuer' in life, or possibly no relationship at all because there is nobody who seems able to guarantee sufficient emotional security. The energy centre of the heart will begin to lower its vibration further with every instance of suppression. Among other things, that will affect the thymus, the heart centre's corresponding endocrine gland, and the heart itself, the corresponding organ. The resulting symptoms could be headaches, circulatory problems, nervous problems, and ultimately heart disease. If the energy suppression is taken to the extreme, the heart centre can block completely, resulting in physical death by heart failure.

Early in such a case, a healer might use the colour green, sounds in the key of F, or Bleeding Heart flower essence since these are some of the subtle energy forces relating to the particular frequency of the energy centre of the heart where it all originated. These influence the heart by bringing it into resonance with them through energy osmosis. Their frequency does not change, but the heart's can.

The life force does not stop flowing until we choose to stop it completely by the will to suppress or resist life. Even that is our own responsibility. We may not notice when our energy system is out of balance because when the energy is blocked from flowing in one centre, it may go to over-energise the others to keep the overall system in balance. In the case of the heart, it might pour to the throat centre where the person would be inclined to talk incessantly in intimate situations to avoid experiencing intimacy or sensations of love that they believe could prove uncomfortable or risky; or alternatively to the solar plexus where intimacy might ignite anger, blame or control tendencies in their behaviour.

These imbalances can be addressed and dis-ease defused if we would only evaluate ourselves in every moment and ask if we are living our truth or not. Are we expressing ourselves in our highest truth and allowing others to do so — without criticism, judgement or resistance? This is very simple but not necessarily the easy road, as it defies many deeply ingrained attitudes and beliefs — the very ones on which the dis-ease is based.

Our expression in life is simply our way of directing the life force. The life force itself is stopped or hindered at its head only by the constraints we put upon our own expression in life. These constraints are due to the underlying restrictive attitudes in our belief system that determine what we judge to be good and bad, right and wrong, acceptable and unacceptable.

Life Force

As we open ourselves to more life-force energy, and to accepting our own and others' heart-felt expressions as perfect and individual, we will turn the whole of our life around and it will begin to look vastly different.

Chapter 11

▲

MASTERY

We've come into this realm to experience a limited version of ourselves called 'physical'. We've become masters of this realm of self-limitation, able to sustain extraordinary pain and struggle. Now it's time to let go of the controls and let the tide turn. It's time to allow the flow of fear to ebb, to embrace our divine mastery, and turn our reality into one of ecstasy and fulfilment.

Humanity has entered a phase of far-reaching change. It is not just transformation. That would be like painting an old house a new colour, making it appear different whilst still actually being the same old place. Neither is it selling out — tossing the baby out with the bathwater by irresponsibly walking away from a house that we've allowed to become a hovel.

This is transmutation — gradually dismantling the house into its constituent materials and using them to construct a totally new one of far superior and more satisfying design, and all the while continuing to live in it!

Nothing at all will go untouched by this tide of change. More and more of us are remembering and recognising ourselves to be the transducers of higher consciousness that we truly are. Every day more people search for answers to questions that have never been addressed by the beliefs of the past. Most people are beginning to explore alternative belief systems which contradict everything that has gone before. Many are already walking out of safe lifestyles and secure jobs to live in new places and by different values.

Alternatives are manifesting as we all direct ever-increasing amounts of energy into the search. New understandings, systems, technologies, information and expertise have appeared, particularly during the past century. In recent decades, new ways of dealing with our lives have developed and become tangible tools, techniques and therapies with which to continue the adaptation process. Though they pushed back the limitations of our understanding and capabilities, we have embraced these contemporary supports and moved beyond even them, only to find newer, more potent ones coming to light in their wake. These send masses of high-frequency ripples through the pool of the consensus reality. Truths are in question as much as falsehoods. Humanity is becoming more and more willing and able to embrace the new consciousness that offers harmony and fulfilment to all, not just some.

Preparation for this shift began thousands of years ago. It gained sudden momentum around two thousand years ago through a man of elevated consciousness who is remembered as Jesus. He spoke of a christ which he promised we would come to know and experience one day. He was actually referring not to himself or any other being, but to christ-consciousness. Christ-consciousness is simply a term given to a particular frequency of the energy of all that is, just as the term 'purple' is given to a particular frequency in our spectrum of visible light, or 'fifty degrees' to a temperature of water. Christ is the name of the frequency of consciousness at which any being ascending from the lower realms, first realises the state of expression and awareness that is pure unconditional love, for themselves and for absolutely all that is. Divine bliss is achieved by anyone who raises their own vibration to match it. It is the rate of vibration in the energy of all that is, that first engenders the pure unshakeable realisation that, in truth, all is unified in that one energy; that nothing is separate from anything else; that every single thing is a fragment of everything else. It is the frequency at which ego as we know it finally dissolves along with all fear, limitation, pain, resistance, control and struggle. Each and every one of us is capable of raising our own frequency to that of christ-consciousness.

Jesus was a highly evolved man, a spiritual master who expounded the virtues of the christ-consciousness in an unenlightened world. He happened to be a physical master who embodied christ-consciousness in absolute purity and expressed his divine truth in his every word and action at a crucial point in our evolution. As a result, people of the time called him Jesus Christ, just as they would have called David who was a farmer, David Farmer. That Jesus lived his higher knowing, that he unwaveringly walked his talk constantly, gave people the impression of his godliness or overt divinity. So much did he inspire and instil love and wonder and faith in people's potential, that he was put on a pedestal and taken out of context — either idolised or feared — by all.

The high-frequency energy of christ-consciousness channelled through Jesus into the earthly realm at a time that began catapulting humankind's consciousness into and through its passing phase to now. That passing evolutionary phase of consciousness was called Piscean. Today, some religious followings still use the symbol of the fish, a carry-over signifying their unwillingness to evolve yet into the christ-consciousness which, ironically, they profess to represent and to honour. Piscean consciousness was a phase of collective mind-consciousness. It brought humankind the experience of group belief systems with their low vibrational fear games of mutual ego validation and control, and disempowerment of the individual through ignorance and irresponsibility. Its purpose was purely to enable the higher mental frequencies of humankind's consciousness to evolve out of simple survival and into a state of discernment, truth and integrity. Out of this growth period would evolve a springboard of love and courage from which the entire species could make the quantum leap into christ-consciousness. Doing so, they would enjoy higher-dimensional realities and capabilities -- higher expressions of life.

But the collective systems of government, religion, culture and nation, race and creed, economy, law, education and medicine, all of which rely on mental will, became increasingly powerful. Although they gained control of the collective consciousness through fear of punishment, scarcity, pain, ignorance, danger, ridicule and invalidation, the overall purpose has been served.

Those were the old ways. They are now dying. All we need do is allow them to pass gracefully. We are now evolving from the old Age of Pisces into the new Age of Aquarius.

The new Aquarian consciousness is individual consciousness. It brings every person the responsibility for consciously expressing and experiencing their own individual spiritual essence — their mastery; their true power as a divine creator of their own reality, in oneness and absolute harmony with all.

Religion is not spirituality, and it seldom, if ever, promotes one's coming into self-power, realisation and godhood. It is another man-made collective which harnesses the power of the masses through a vice-like grip of fear and control in order to benefit a select few, doing so by spreading sophisticated smoke screens of complication, esoteric ritual and downright superstition to keep the average person, as well as most of their own clergy, from the truth (if they themselves ever knew it in the first place). That grip is now weakening in favour of true spirituality.

Spirituality unconditionally honours each individual's divine uniqueness and right to reclaim their mastery in the way that is true to them, and at the time that they are ready. Without exception, anything that contradicts any person's sense of self-power and reinforces their victim belief is not purely spiritually based and will crumble through this period of self-realisation. Everything that consciously or subconsciously attracts individuals into a collective system to control their beliefs about themselves, or tells them what they must or must not believe or do, will dissolve through transmutation. Be it personal and individual, or mutual and collective, everything that represents structure, inflexibility and disallowance will crumble. This could sound like some kind of retribution, but it is not. In fact, the contrary is more accurate.

The upward shift in consciousness is a well-deserved prize after a prolonged period of self-limiting experience in the dense, third-dimensional material realm. Those who choose to try and perpetuate the fear-based systems of control and power-mongery through the changes will not be judged as bad or wrong; they will simply experience increasingly traumatic feelings every time something goes out of control for them. Trying to resist the changes and control them to meet preconceptions of safety or predictability is really only an attempt to maintain fear consciousness and a reality of limitation, pain and struggle. What's more, it is pitting oneself against the flow of the entire cosmos, against All-That-Is. A hopeless and fruitless task, not unlike an ant trying to change the direction in which an elephant is walking. Little wonder there is such frustration, confusion, uncertainty and sense of helplessness in these times.

But the beauty is that we can use the whole experience as the most clear and direct guidance possible because, if it appears traumatic, we will know that our consciousness is still attached to our ego's polarity view; if our sensation of it all is relative calmness and detachment, we will know that we are up with the play.

Once we sit back and enjoy the ride, we will begin to see a new reality form; one created with the energy that had previously been focused upon the maintenance of pain, dis-ease, scarcity, struggle, resistance, control, insecurity, poverty, fear, war, hatred and starvation. All the symptoms of polarity consciousness will disintegrate. As we invoke the higher frequencies of energy, it will evoke its characteristics of love, abundance, harmony, peace, well-being, comfort, absolute beauty and fulfilment for all who choose to move with it.

This whole shift in consciousness is being managed and facilitated by a host of unconditionally-loving beings who are not even in our dimensional reality. They are the beings already residing in the higher dimensions whom we had asked to remind us when we were about to suffocate from lack of love in the depths of physicality. Some might think of them as spirit guides, or spirit helpers, others as Archangels or Angels, Universal and Cosmic Beings, Brotherhoods and Councils of Divine Beings in Light, Star Beings, The Elohim, Ascended Masters or even God. Though we may not often realise it, they carefully help each of us absorb understanding and knowledge in the perfect ways at the perfect times so that we might evolve into ecstatic fulfilment. They are now guiding us to integrate more and more high-frequency love-consciousness into our lives.

Their guidance has never faltered throughout time,

and they have made their presence felt and heard by channelling their wisdom and love as purely as human circumstances allowed. They did so through numerous high-consciousness people who have walked the physical Earth in all civilisations and races. Such renowned and conscious masters as Ahknaton, Buddha, Confucius, Jesus, Kokopelli, Krishna, Kwan Yin, Lao Tzu, Mahavira, Mohammed, Montezuma, Quetzalcoatl, Luther and Socrates were among those who played a part in nudging their respective cultures forward into higher states of understanding. They expressed their own mastery so that we could all make this evolutionary quantum leap today. They did so by allowing the christ frequency of the life force to flow through them in their words as well as their actions, thereby truly representing and demonstrating the christ potential within us all here on Earth.

Now, we are all being asked to do the same as those masters did. Not just say as they said, in the fashion of so many cultural and religious followings of today, but to do as they did; to be now harbingers of high consciousness, self-realisation and change, as they were then.

They knew a divine master resided in each of us, and that some day we would know it too. Let's not disappoint them. Let's show them — and ourselves — that we are capable and willing to rise to the occasion; to take up the mantle of a christ-conscious species creating a reality based on unconditional love.

Christ-consciousness is unconditional love — absolutely allowing everyone and everything to just be without putting any ifs, buts, maybes, shoulds, ought-tos or other controlling conditions on our allowance of them. When Jesus said that, until christ has reached the four corners of the Earth, mankind will not enter the Kingdom of Heaven, he was not asking for Christianity to be taken to all parts of the planet and forced down people's throats by missionaries, mercenaries or self-appointed do-gooders. That is not loving and divine as he taught: it is a manipulative, fear-driven religious system's convenient interpretation used to gain control of the minds, hearts, lives and spirituality of the people. No. It simply meant that, not until all humanity allows its collective consciousness to rise into the christ frequency, will we have manifested a life of absolute unconditional love, peace, harmony and ecstatic fulfilment for ourselves to experience. And this is happening right now as the entire human race transmutes the limited versions of itself that have been the reality of the past, into self-realised masters who will co-create an entirely new reality.

These times call upon us all to begin thinking, speaking, acting and living a new truth — unconditional love; unconditional allowance. We're asked to live it totally — to be it, full time, every second; every thought we have, every breath we take, every move we make. It is now our turn to demonstrate and live such divine power through love, not control, rather than give up the responsibility once again to someone outside ourselves to live it for us.

We are equal to those masters who came to remind us. They have all said so themselves. They knew we were as divine as them. They have taught us to walk, and now it is graduation time — it's time for us to stand up and show that we've been listening. It's time for us all to walk our own talk, rather than someone else's; to discern our own truth, listen to it and live it, knowing that with each step we take in that truth, the voice will become louder and clearer, and it will lead us closer to absolute blissful fulfilment and mastery.

Figure 11.1

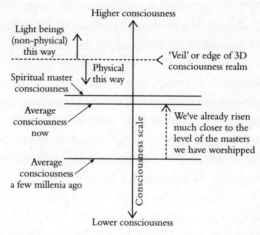

We are all now becoming clearer channels for our own higher knowing to pour through, just as those great figures were in their times. Their teachings and abilities, though different in their manifestations to each other's, were the same consciousness. It was just their unique, individualised life-expression to which they remained true. Their understandings were strange and difficult to digest for the vast majority of the population of the time (Figure 11.1). So is everything that is coming into our awareness now. More and more people are unable to reconcile what they see in our world with what they are holding as their deepest truths about themselves and their fellow souls in embodiment.

Just as a droplet of water does not know when it is part of an enormous tidal wave, so it is that much of humankind has not yet realised that we have been on the move for ages, and that the wave of en-light-enment is gaining momentum now, increasing in its magnitude and speed. As we become more able to assimilate greater knowledge and understanding, it is gradually being released to us so that we become more aware of the wave and the part each of us plays within it.

In keeping with our shift to personal power and responsibility, the truth is entering through our own personal channels, rather than those outside us. Every one of us is being asked to listen to and trust our own inner voice so that we can be guided through the distractions, the mis-truths and the changes in ways that are different and perfect for each one of us. The unfolding of events will render the old world so obsolete that we won't even be able to recall it.

Just take a last look at the way the world has been and appreciate it for the purpose it has served. Then turn around and revel in anticipation of the wonder and ecstasy that awaits as we all move into a new world of such beauty, vitality and fulfilment that we cannot presently even begin to imagine, let alone describe.

Chapter 12

▲

REUNION

The frequency of the energy of humankind's consciousness is now ascending at an accelerating rate. As it does so, we will see and experience the most profound changes on our planet, in our lives, and within humanity and ourselves. There are no intellectual explanations; we must experience it to understand. There is no proof because it is self-realisation by trust and allowance, and getting there is its only proof. Nothing whatsoever can stop this, and nothing whatsoever will remain untouched by it.

The tide has turned for some, is still turning for others, and is about to turn for the remainder. Many already see the reality changing as their experience of life is changing completely. Some things are appearing to be the same as they were but are being experienced differently. Other things are changing before our eyes, requiring that we experience them in new ways with new measures and values. All aspects of life are opening up to a greater range of options so that we can learn to exercise discernment and take responsibility for the choices we make.

Our entire world is heading into an all-pervading shake-up, and nobody is coming to rescue us. It is our own responsibility to enable it to happen as smoothly and easily as possible. This will be achieved by us all becoming constantly in honour of our own truth — in our thoughts and feelings, responses and actions — in absolutely every instant. We can talk, think, theorise, teach and own it to our heart's content, but until we *be* it in action, it will prove to be just as traumatic for us as for those who choose to ignore it completely. We must all get out of our heads, into our hearts, and into action immediately if we are to enjoy a beautiful, enlightening and enlivening experience.

We are transmuting our reality by choosing to change the manifested form of the very energy of which it is essentially created. We can only achieve this vast, exquisite feat by being the divine master-creators that we truly are in our density of experience. It is imperative that each of us remembers and expresses that Mastery which we have denied for lifetimes, having hidden it under such a heavy blanket of fear. That is how we will move out of the fear and transmute the energies that are our responsibility — our own creations.

Inevitably, this transmutation is bringing about innumerable structural changes, the effects of which will be felt throughout our reality. Its physical effects will be to release the energies that are held in low-frequency form into an increasingly high-frequency configuration. Since lower vibrations of the energy determine the more solid or static forms, then the most solid and inflexible structures of our conscious reality will feel the greatest impact. The more rigid or inflexible any manifestation is, the more impact it will experience through the shift. That applies to beliefs, thoughts and emotions as well as physical bodies, objects and the environment. Straight lines and sharp corners are manifestations of control, rigidity and fear-consciousness; round corners, and curved and free-form lines are manifestations of allowance and love-consciousness. Look around yourself and your world and you'll quickly get an idea of where the greatest impacts will be felt in the environment!

Any person with an inflexible, controlling or judgemental tendency will feel the impact more than one who is loving and allowing at all times. Most cultures, nations and social systems have inflexible or judgemental tendencies, with many rules and controls. Those who perpetrate that tendency or support it through their own belief system and actions will automatically feel the impact more greatly than anyone who is indifferent towards that particular belief structure. For example, if a country believes in the need to persecute, manipulate, or heavily legislate to maintain power and control, then that country and its people will need to stretch further to embrace the new reality of higher-frequency love consciousness that is pouring in to depose the old. Those which have more flexible and allowing systems in place will find it easier. Equally, a person who has a strong belief in what is right and wrong or good and bad, and can't see past such judgement, will find the change much more difficult to accept than the person who is allowing and accepting of the foibles, differences and idiosyncrasies of others.

The effect on anyone holding attachments to

traditional, physical reality and the way things were, will be far more intense and disruptive than on those who are prepared to look forward and embrace an alternative. Those who can see no other feasible way to find fulfilling experience in life but through control and manipulation will experience their entire life going out of control. And indeed it will be going out of control. Actually, it will be going out of fear. Simultaneously, it will be going into love and into a loving and abundant reality for all.

On a personal scale, the fact that the whole physical energy is ascending in frequency means that more than our non-physical consciousness will be changing. It is the very energy that makes up the atoms, molecules, cells, tissues and organs of our bodies, so they will be changing too.

As they raise their vibration, the effect will be to expand their capability of absorbing the energies of love and joy in the form of Divine Light. Most of us will experience dramatic physical effect from the influx of extreme joy — spontaneous and inexplicable tears or laughter may punctuate life as we transduce the incoming energy and transmute the old. That is a sign that we are not able to assimilate that degree of cosmic love without sending our body into reactions of some sort. Imagine, then, being exposed to joyous experiences of even greater intensity, and on a permanent basis! It would be downright immobilising for us — we'd be unable to go about our lives for uncontrollable laughter, tears of joy, or bodily convulsions of ecstatic rapture. That is why the cells in our bodies need to modify, so that they will be able to absorb and maintain far higher energies. This will bring us rapidly into the need to re-learn our long-lost natural abilities to sustain these higher energies and high sensitivity experiences, such as through regular meditation. That way, the unfamiliar and intense feelings of the higher expressions of love, to which we are initially unable to relate, won't disable us.

At cellular level, this process will manifest for each of us as the release of the physical symptoms of our old beliefs which are held as dis-ease and toxins in our bodies. These can be mental, emotional or physical. The transmutation will happen at the rate each of us chooses to let the beliefs and attachments of our old way of existing and experiencing dissolve away, and allow ourselves to experience stronger feelings and sensations.

Imagine someone unaware of bicycles who suddenly finds themselves materialised on one, freewheeling down a beautiful country lane on a gloriously sunny day. A lovely fresh breeze is in their face and they do not have a care in the practical world. Unfortunately, being unfamiliar with bicycles, they would probably not appreciate this as the joyous, exhilarating, liberating feeling that many cyclists would. In fact it could feel quite the opposite! Unfamiliar and upsetting feelings of helplessness, fear and distress could arise as they felt unable to control the contraption! And all over what regular cyclists would likely consider a delightful experience.

Similarly, when exposed to higher vibrational energy, strong and unfamiliar feelings can manifest in the body.

Among other things, it can make the heart pound, the pulse rise, the mind race, and perspiration to flow, as though distress was setting in. Our controlling, fear-logic reaction to such unfamiliar feelings is to stop them happening — resist the circumstances, stop the experience, quell the symptoms. But no! There is no need to panic or worry. These are not symptoms of dis-ease. They are sensations of energy that is flowing at a rate with which you are not familiar. Many people are experiencing such things and, mistaking sensations in their body for symptoms, they habitually seek medical treatment to suppress it. Instead, allow yourself to adapt to them — allow them to flow. Drink them in and in no time you'll not feel them that way any more. Your body will have acclimatised and they'll be feelings of rapture and thrill.

It is only when the life-force energy is not flowing that we don't feel. But when life force is not flowing we don't live either. To try and stop feeling is to try and stop living! To avoid feelings that may arise from new experience is to avoid life itself.

Now is the time for us all to move out of this fear of life, this victim mentality that has trapped us in prisons of self-limitation for millennia. Now is the time to live life, not resist it; to understand our strongest feelings as being signs that we are contributing to the transmutation of the consciousness for the highest good of all.

In such feelings, we are performing our divine spiritual mission at last — to wake up and step into our spiritual roles in the ultimate plan of humanity's evolution out of the dense material plane and into the realms of Light — from atoms to angels.

That is what we are being called to do through this most crucial time in the entire history of humankind. The higher frequencies are being fed to us gradually, enabling our fear-based, structurally-limiting reality to dissolve as gently as possible and dovetail into a love-based, flowing, fulfilling one.

This de-structuring and transmutation affects not only our species but our space–time continuum as well. Our whole physical reality and everything in it is created and perpetuated by our own thoughts and beliefs, and neither space nor time are exceptions.

Time, as we experience it in 3D, is linear — it flows from the past into the present and on into the future in a continuous time line. This enables us to experience consequence — cause-and-effect. Linear time is just a manifestation of our thoughts being projected, both consciously and unconsciously, outside our 'now' moment into the past and the future. This happens through memory and expectation respectively. These projections of thought are yet another aspect of fear-consciousness, and the need to control life to be safe and predictable. The extent to which humanity's thoughts go outside the 'now' moment is the extent to which our ego's fearful consciousness traps us into living by consequence — today as a consequence of yesterday; tomorrow a consequence of today. They are another avenue by which we diminish our power and manifest pain on the mental, emotional and physical levels. They also demonstrate yet again the ego's belief in the need for control to ensure safety and predictability.

From a spiritual viewpoint the thoughts of past and future take us out of alignment with ourselves 'now'. They put us in a position of doing things to occupy time, instead of simply being. The part of our consciousness that functions emotionally lives in the past, remembering what experiences felt like. The part that functions mentally lives in the future, worrying and trying to manipulate and control the flow of life to ensure we only encounter good experiences. Together, they disable us from being — from experiencing 'now' — for fear of what the truth of this moment might feel like.

However, we cannot actually be any other time than right now. Neither can we be any other place than right here.

Here and now is where and when our physical bodies are being, living in a constant flow of present instants. We just don't see and experience it that way.

Since we can only be here and now, until we come into alignment by focusing our emotional energy (feelings) and mental energy (thoughts) totally in every moment, and act accordingly here and now, we will continue to dissipate our life force. We will continue to feel powerless and vulnerable through being disconnected from the full power of our true selves, instead our energy being spread out and drained into somewhere and sometime that we actually are not, rendering it unrecognisable and almost useless to us. We will also continue to manifest in our physical reality the uncomfortable symptoms of ego run amuck. Such symptoms stem from the ego's misguided belief that we are actually able to live outside our 'now', and in so doing gain enough control of life to allay all fears.

Time is only something our fearful ego desires to gain control over in an effort to make life safe and predictable, though it was always going to be perfect anyway. As our consciousness shifts into higher frequencies, more of our energy will be redirected into the experience of now, and less into the past and future. We will then learn to love and allow every moment we are in. This requires that we cease both guilt and worry in their myriad forms. Thereby we will direct more attention into each moment rather than resisting or avoiding it. This will empower our every 'now' moment to contain more life force through our redirected emotional and mental energy. We will regain our sense of power and command over our own lives, dissolving fears and limitations in the process. More significantly, as we divert the energy by our thoughts, from the past and future into now, we will disable the creation of linear time as we know it. If yesterday and tomorrow cannot be created, they cannot be experienced. If it is no longer being created and we are no longer experiencing it, then it is no longer a part of our reality. The time factor of our reality, as we presently experience it, will consequently dissolve for us. We will be living in the cosmic 'now' — an eternal life with no sense of the passage of time (Figure 12.1).

Space is what ego's polarity consciousness has used to perpetuate our belief in being separate — from every

Figure 12.1

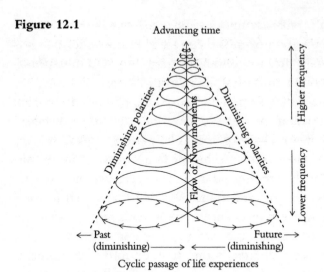

Cyclic passage of life experiences

thing and every one. It too shall be dissolving. As we channel in and assimilate more and more higher vibrational energy, raising our conscious understanding and awareness, the allowance of the 'now' will nurture the consciousness of unity with everything that exists in the moment. As this awareness grows, so will our thoughts of oneness, and we will be feeding less and less energy to our fading ego-belief in separateness. Separateness experiences will diminish as the thoughts that created them are replaced by thoughts of absolute oneness with all. Thus, the space that is created to house the old separateness manifestations will diminish along with it. We will be living in the cosmic 'here' — an eternity of simply being; omnipresence, affording no sense of separateness from anything.

The way each person experiences this dramatic and

radical transmutation of consciousness and realities will be absolutely unique, and equally indescribable and euphoric for one as for another. But however it manifests, it is leading each of us out of our self-inflicted spiritual isolation and back to our origins. As with any prolonged sojourn from what we consider home, we will revive memories and feel a growing anticipation, joy and sense of familiarity and belonging throughout the return journey.

Chapter 13

▲

FULFILMENT

*The rise in frequency of our consciousness is the
acceleration of the vibrational rate of the energy of all that
is in our reality. Through it, we will have come out of fear
and into love, while at the same time coming out of the
third dimension into our higher-dimensional origins,
carrying within us all the experience we have gathered.
Most importantly, we will have remained conscious and
fully aware throughout the entire journey.*

This global dissolving of our reality is actually only a
symptom of us moving back through the veil we created
so long ago (Figure 13.1). Through this ascension in the
vibration of the all-pervading energy, every single atomic
particle that constructs our world and our bodies will
gradually change to a higher energy state. We will remain
fully aware of these changes, experiencing many new,
powerful and vitalising sensations as they continue to
unfold.

We can't begin to imagine what life would be like in
the eternal 'here' and 'now' because our present
consciousness is still unable to relate to it. And we don't
need to. A time will simply come when we will look at
ourselves and each other, at our lives and our world, and

see it all totally transformed — even the things and conditions we'd never have thought possible. We will be having an entirely different experience of life as we reside in a reality of vastly higher vibrational energy with consciousness of vastly higher frequencies. Our reality will be one without the limitations we presently think of as being normal, necessary, natural and immutable. It will be a life of high energy; a life of lightness, freedom, love and fulfilment.

Figure 13.1

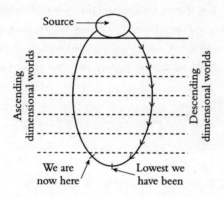

Instantaneous manifestation, telepathic communication, teleportation at will, and eternal life — immortality — are destined to be ours. These are not dreams: they are natural attributes of the higher vibrational realities from which we descended for this physical experience; those to which we are now returning.

Consider sound for example. It requires a physical substance such as air or water to carry its waves. The spoken word is a physical 3D form of communication which takes time to send and space for the carrier-substance to occupy. In the higher planes, because such dense substances can't exist, all communication takes place through the non-physical vibrations of energy by thought transfer which is instantaneous. This is telepathy. Similarly, manifestation will become instantaneous since the energy is more malleable and will not take the time to form that it takes in the density of 3D. That will enable our thoughts to manifest in the moment we have them. What's more, if our thoughts are at another situation, we will be able to dematerialise here and rematerialise there in an instant, teleporting in for the experience. Everyone will gain these abilities automatically as a result of their evolution in consciousness, not by extra-sensory party tricks, or even by some exclusive psychic ability supposedly reserved for only a few special people.

Every culture on our planet has at some time had a belief system which alluded to these changes for all humanity, with promises of heralding the manifestation of our divinity. Armageddon, End of the World, Doomsday, Judgement Day, Utopia, Nirvana, the Promised Land, the Last Day, Dream Time, Heaven on Earth, and the In-breath of God are some of the terms used to identify it. They are all just different names for the same event — releasing one reality for another; displacing the old limited way of life by allowing a new and fulfilling one to manifest in its place; one of ecstasy, unconditional love and mutual conscious Mastery.

Now, you might begin to ask 3D questions like 'Will

I still have my body? What about my cat? My home and my loved ones? Friends and family?' There is nothing wrong with these questions because they all deserve answers to help dissolve fear and doubt in our consciousness. But such thoughts only originate from our existing consciousness, which is still attached to physicality through the ego. That consciousness is undergoing an unimaginable overhaul so that it can absorb and relate to more energy — more love, light and allowance — more life. It truly doesn't matter whether present Earthly things will be there in our new reality or not, because by the time we reach such choices, everyone's consciousness (including the cat's!) will have risen to a level that is irrelevant to our present state. We will no longer have such attachments based on need and separation which generate the belief in loss and the experience of it. It is presently impossible for us to fully appreciate the difference, since our present consciousness cannot expand to encompass that range of energy frequencies — we are still so limited. Suffice to say, we will be in an unconditionally loving state of being, and our relationships with our bodies, lovers, friends, family, possessions, beliefs, pets — indeed our entire reality — will be totally different from our present experiences and understandings. They will be absolutely fulfilling in every way. We will instantly manifest whatever we choose to experience, whenever and wherever we choose.

Throughout this process our attachment to all previously created and accepted comfort zones will be challenged over and over. No sooner will we have become comfortable with new experiences and understandings than we'll be needing to relinquish them for another set of even higher frequency. As we become capable of more, so it will come to us. The further we progress, the more farcical, unsatisfactory, limiting and impossible the past reality (the one we are experiencing now) will seem. What we experience as the best of times now will fall off the bottom end of the scale and seem like the worst, as we progress through such highly love-charged realities. So will the new 'good times' quickly become comparatively dull and dissatisfying until we have shifted completely into the next higher octave of ecstatic existence.

Think of it as though we are going through a filter. To revisit the ice, water and steam analogy, a block of ice would represent the dense forms of congested, resistant thoughts, attitudes and emotions in our fear-consciousness. They cannot make it through the filter. But they can flow through as water, leaving behind any dense 'lumps' of energy on the way. So we need to heal, or melt away, all of our dense energies — our toxic fear- and control-based mental, emotional and physical pollutants — the self-limiting thoughts, beliefs, attitudes, emotions, attachments, and physical dis-ease that have been such a familiar part of our 3D lives. To do so, we just need to become more fluid and flexible in our beliefs and attitudes about life, our reality and our Selves. That means more loving and allowing.

Remember, this is not being forced upon us. It is a cosmic gift of immeasurable proportion, beauty and fulfilment that humanity has worked towards for aeons without realising. We will have choice every step of the way and, knowing it, we will be making our choices increasingly from love, not fear. It is all managed with absolute precision through the infinitely loving guidance of our own Higher Selves, Angelic Realms and the Divine Beings in the higher dimensions of Light. These are not 'dead people' but forms of intelligence that have chosen never to descend into the unconsciousness of gross material form. They reside in and know only the dimensions of conscious bliss which are above ours. Together, they endeavour to impart inspired wisdom and understanding to all of us, facilitating the progressively faster ascension of our vibration.

This ascension of consciousness is now enabling us all to continuously experience the sensations resulting from gradually dissolving our self-limiting thought forms concerning what is in our lives, and our emotional attachments to it all. It is enabling us to embrace unconditional love at a perfect rate that won't overwhelm us and render us unconscious. This way, we will progressively transmute what we are being into a higher expression of consciousness.

Historically, this gradual change has been compressed into the single sudden release of limitation which manifested as physical death. But this time, we need not lose consciousness and find ourselves 'on the other side'. It is as though the instant of reclaimed freedom that has been labelled 'death' (which is actually just the death of one reality in order to experience another) is being stretched out over many years and exceeded, enabling us to revel in the release of our limitations and the return to our full divine power and wholeness. We will maintain our consciousness throughout the transmutation process over these years, experiencing all of the ecstatic changes and releases of density and limitation as we surrender to this monumental shift in realities.

By the time it has come to pass, we will most likely not even notice. We will be in an entirely new reality; the result of a prolonged stream of change. The past will be irrelevant, if not forgotten completely. We will have moved through what was the veil of forgetfulness and into the higher dimensions of consciousness, mastering all their inherent remarkable abilities along the way.

Though everyone has the choice at every instant, some may find it too difficult to relinquish old belief systems and attachments to past experiences, thoughts, attitudes and feelings. But all those who choose to take responsibility, be courageous and let themselves experience their own way through it, will realise an immeasurable ecstasy that will become constant, not temporary — like a sexual orgasm that never stops; exhilaration that goes on for ever.

Only positive, beautiful, loving, supportive, harmonious thought and attitude will activate the new Light and manifest for all. The old low-vibrational consciousness will not, and will de-manifest as a result. Those who are still entrenched in and attached to the fear, pain, lack, guilt, judgement, dependency and struggle will see their reality falling apart before their very eyes. If they choose not to release their addiction to such self-limitation and negativity, their entire world will dissolve without them becoming a part of the new one manifesting. It will be the end of their world, with both it and them passing into the Source energy of all that is, releasing both density and conscious identity to melt into the pure energy from which they had descended into their own stream of conscious being. Once more they will be integrated with the infinite ocean of original energy in service to the eternal process of Creation throughout all that is, never having experienced the incomprehensibly ecstatic rapture derived from consciously reclaiming their mastery and rediscovering their own light — their infinite beauty, magnificence and divinity; their godhood — as the rest will.

Ascension brings the release of all toxins and pollutants in our bodies and energy fields through transmutation. That means letting go of all fear-based beliefs and thoughts, and consciously creating love-based ones with the same thought energy. This happens through changing one's mind about the prevailing reality. Its overall result will be a world reflecting to us the absence of pollutants and toxins. It is the sublime dove-tailing of two vastly different realities. The Mayan and Hopi Indians, Aborigines and ancient Egyptians, to name just a few, have had knowledge and a clear understanding of such a monumental event in humankind's future history. They are even consistent regarding its apparent conclusion — as we move into the second decade of this new millennium. To enable it to be gradual, enlightening and ecstatic for us, rather than traumatic, it will require the time that is left between now and then.

Remember, each of us is manifesting our own life and we do have the choice to create and live in a reality of a totally different nature. Our entire world of experience is transmuting through our own consciousness, birthing into a higher octave of energy — a loving, ecstatic, abundant and peaceful reality — a veritable Heaven on Earth. We're going home.

To contribute in our own perfect way, we need only take the courage to listen to our own inner truth and be absolutely devoted to that truth in every instant without hesitation or fear of consequence; to acknowledge our individual, beautiful, perfectly Divine Selves and allow them to just be, shining in every way, radiating unconditional love in every thought, in every action, in every moment.

That is where you fit in.

EXPERIMENTAL WORKSHOPS

Paul Walsh-Roberts presents workshops, seminars and services around the world which actualise the principles of this book in the daily lives of everyone who attends. The workshops include:

COSMIC ACTIVATION
Opening Your Channels to Higher Light

Get in touch with your own Inner Guidance and the Masters in Light who are in service to humanity at these crucial times. Experience the tangible physical effects of high-frequency energy and learn how to use and direct it at will for guidance, vitality and inspiration, and for healing and vocal/written channelling.

LIGHTBODY HEALING
Self-healing on all Levels

Use your subtle energy bodies to transmute your own physical, emotional and mental healing issues with speed and ease. Be in service to the whole of humanity, as well as Mother Earth. Learn a powerful, rapid and effective way of transmuting the effects of the Human Ascension in your own daily life.

MANIFESTATION
Creating the Life You Long For

Learn to identify existing manifestation in your daily

life and redirect your creative forces into increasingly fulfilling experiences for yourself as well as for all humankind. Contribute in tangible ways to the co-creation of Heaven on Earth.

If you'd like information about either Paul or his wife Alexandria and the life enhancement and spiritual empowerment workshops, seminars and consultations each conducts around the world, please visit **www.lovenlight.net** where you'll also discover how you can participate directly in the global healing and consciousness shift. If you'd like to know their timetables of activities or to bring their work to your area, then e-mail **mastery@lovenlight.net** directly.